HOW · TO · BE
ALONE

HOW · TO · BE
ALONE

IF YOU WANT TO, AND EVEN IF YOU DON'T

LANE MOORE

ATRIA PAPERBACK

New York   London   Toronto   Sydney   New Delhi

ATRIA
PAPERBACK

An Imprint of Simon & Schuster, Inc.
1230 Avenue of the Americas
New York, NY 10020

First Atria Paperback edition November 2018

ATRIA PAPERBACK and colophon are trademarks of Simon & Schuster, Inc.

For information about special discounts for bulk purchases, please contact Simon & Schuster Special Sales at 1-866-506-1949 or business@simonandschuster.com.

The Simon & Schuster Speakers Bureau can bring authors to your live event. For more information or to book an event, contact the Simon & Schuster Speakers Bureau at 1-866-248-3049 or visit our website at www.simonspeakers.com.

Interior design by Amy Trombat

Manufactured in the United States of America

10 9 8 7 6 5 4 3 2 1

Library of Congress Cataloging-in-Publication Data

Names: Moore, Lane, author.
Title: How to be alone : if you want to, and even if you don't / Lane Moore.
Description: First Atria Paperback edition. | New York : Atria Paperback, 2018.
Identifiers: LCCN 2018023366 (print) | LCCN 2018034666 (ebook) | ISBN 9781501178849 (ebook) | ISBN 9781501178832 (paperback)
Subjects: LCSH: Moore, Lane. | Comedians--United States--Biography. | Women comedians--United States--Biography. | Love--Humor. | LCGFT: Autobiographies. | Humor.
Classification: LCC PN2287.M696 (ebook) | LCC PN2287.M696 A3 2018 (print) | DDC 792.702/8092 [B] --dc23
LC record available at https://lccn.loc.gov/2018023366

ISBN 978-1-5011-7883-2
ISBN 978-1-5011-7884-9 (ebook)

Dedicated to the following, in no particular order:

Fiona Apple, Stevie Nicks, Nina Simone, Diana Ross, the Cranberries, Dolores O'Riordan, Garbage, PJ Harvey, Sarah McLachlan, *Romy and Michele's High School Reunion*, *The Craft*, *Scream*, Letters to Cleo, *Living Single*, Moonpools & Caterpillars, *Harold and Maude*, *Strangers with Candy*, *Mr. Show*, Janeane Garofalo, Marya Hornbacher, Lauryn Hill, Selena, Alanis Morissette, Ani DiFranco, the Cure, *Wonderfalls*, Sheryl Crow, Dinah Washington, Sinéad O'Connor, Cyndi Lauper, John Waters, Prince, *Reality Bites*, Lesley Gore, the Dixie Chicks, *Matilda*, *Girl, Interrupted*, Julie Doiron, Winona Ryder, Patty Griffin, Patti Smith, Mazzy Star, the Crystals, Tori Amos, *Wet Hot American Summer*, Michael Showalter, Michael Ian Black, *A League of Their Own*, Angelina Jolie, Sandra Bullock, *Practical Magic*, *Anne of Green Gables*, *10 Things I Hate About You*, Brittany Murphy, Natalie Imbruglia, Poe, Ella Fitzgerald, Radiohead, Sam Phillips, Neko Case, Kathleen Edwards, Faith Hill, Gin Blossoms, Better Than Ezra, Cameron Crowe, the Go-Go's, No Doubt, Heart, Portishead, *Late Night with Conan O'Brien*, Amy Poehler, Depeche Mode, Aretha Franklin, Cat Power, Bic Runga, Debbie Harry, Parker Posey, *The Breakfast Club*, *Empire Records*, *Veronica Mars*, *Buffy the Vampire Slayer*, *Arrested Development*, Deana Carter, Shania Twain, Jo Dee Messina, Patsy Cline, Margaret Cho, and Rosie O'Donnell.

And the small voice in my head that never let me give up.

CONTENTS

EMERGENCY CONTACT LEFT BLANK

Let me tell you this: If you meet a loner, no matter
what they tell you, it's not because they enjoy solitude.
It's because they have tried to blend into the world
before, and people continue to disappoint them.

—JODI PICOULT, *MY SISTER'S KEEPER*

The first time I remember describing my family as "nonexistent" was in middle school, when I described myself as "the asexual offspring of a tree" in an attempt to make total abandonment, in the face of very alive parents, sound super chill.

There's a very particular sort of no-man's-land that comes with having alive parents who are technically there, could technically take you in if you really needed somewhere to go, but if you went there, you wouldn't be any safer than anywhere else.

Now, you might be reading this and thinking, "But my family is so wonderful, and I still feel alone," or "My mom sucks, but my dad was so awesome, but I still feel lonely all the time," or "My mom was the best person, and ever since she died, I feel so lonely," and to those people I will say, I have no idea what any of that must feel like. None. Not a clue.

Even now, as I sit here writing this, I have never felt loved, in the way I imagine many of you have, in my entire life. I know that sounds depressing, so don't worry; my brain has responded accordingly by being depressed. I wish I had felt loved. It seems pretty cool. That isn't to say I haven't had glimpses of what it might be like: the equivalent of shitty little face-mask samples from Sephora—just enough to cover your forehead and part of your right cheek. Just enough to give you an idea of how great it could be if there had been more of it for a longer period of time—enough for several uses, maybe even a lifetime of them. But the larger sizes are pricey and out of stock, and it's fine, you didn't need it anyway. You'd gone this long without it.

I wish I could give you a clean and simple business card explaining what happened so I could be the kind of orphan who would immediately make sense to everyone. Like if my parents had a socially recognizable problem that immediately explained their inability to take care of me and my sister. Something I could put on paper and hand to people as proof. *Here. This is why.* And then I could write those two paragraphs for you, easy. Example: "I have a cocaine-addicted dad and a mom who loved meth!" Boom, no further details required, let's move on to the jokes! But they don't. And it's not that simple.

If you tell someone your parent is an alcoholic or an addict, they seemingly, on some level, get that you had a rough childhood. You don't need to expand for hours, trying to prove your case like a lawyer with the odds stacked against him. Or in some cases spend your whole life trying to figure out if, wait a minute, holy shit, your parents actually *were* toxic after all, like you're trapped inside a one-player game of Clue and the big mystery is "Why am I like this?" You're immediately seen and heard and validated and everything you see is real—or so I imagine. Similarly, if you know someone's medical diagnosis, this affords you the ability to say, "Yeah, my dad's a schizophrenic," and people will at least reply, "Oh, shit," and trust you and move on—and maybe even google "schizophrenia" later that night and continue muttering their *whoa*s on their own time. When it's not that simple, or you don't have any of that information, it's that much easier to go your whole life thinking it's just *you*; you're too sensitive, you're wrong, you need too much, you could fix your relationship with them if you wanted to, if you would just do the right thing, whatever that is, only God knows, but you should die trying.

My favorite response whenever I tell people I don't really have a family is "But what about your grandparents?" or "But what about your siblings?"—a bizarre move on their part to assume I actually have, like, twenty relatives who love and support me and I just didn't look hard enough for them. "Missed a spot!" Except the spot is a reliable, healthy caretaker of any kind. Trust me, I wish I could spin blindfolded and point to one to appease you and me, but I promise, there's no one to point to.

My extended family exists, and I passively love most of them in the same way you might if you saw a childhood teacher at the grocery store who always seemed nice enough.

I knew them growing up and I've seen their photos in photo albums and I know they know who I am and I know what they do for work. Kind of. But mostly I just see them as people who could've saved me and didn't. But then I think, Maybe they didn't know how bad it was, I wasn't technically their problem, etc., etc., forever; that desperation to believe that the people who hurt you didn't know, had a rough day, aren't bad people, that it was all a misunderstanding. And if they knew what they did or didn't do, they'd say sorry. They would.

I grew up a real-life Matilda: surrounded by biological family who, in constantly rotating ways, couldn't be bothered. I can see all of the origin stories of my family members now and can empathize with them, understand the reasons why things played out that way. But as a child, I just wanted my parents to live somewhere else without my ever knowing they existed so I could firmly be what I already was, albeit not legally, albeit not technically, albeit not on the surface: alone in a way you can never quite describe to people. But I'll try.

In the very, very earliest years of my life, maybe around five, I remember my mom telling me she believed in me. I don't remember what it felt like, but I can see it in pictures, and remember it in that hazy way you remember things from when you were too young to remember things. My mom loved me. And in the years that followed, she became so shattered from my dad's abuse, as we all had, that it was like she was dead. So the only voices in my head were my dad breaking me down to nothing and stepping on the pieces, and the constant fear I would die, we would all die, whenever he felt it was time. And even though my mom didn't have the same kind of viciousness, no one in my family was supplying any alternative views on my worthiness either.

I reached out to my mom and my sister at the end of writing this book, and I can see now the truth of what happened to all of us was heartbreaking. My mom (and later my sister) coped with my dad's maliciousness by leaving her own body and mind, resurfacing only to, as if possessed, repeat many of the same things he'd said and done to her, to us. They don't remember most of it, which for years I thought, *Bullshit.* But the more I talk to the women in my family, the more I know they truly don't remember a lot, and they are horrified they passed on his behaviors. And I understand that because I don't remember a lot. But I remember more than they do, even though I wish I didn't. I say this because it is essential to me to convey the shattering I feel in my chest when I think of your holding my father and mother in the same camp. Because they are absolutely not.

Calling my mom and my sister was the first time I was able to release some of the anger I had, instead of living in a constantly conflicted state because they were victims of the same abuse I was, they just handled it in a different way, so could I be angry at them, even though they were victims too? Was it cruel to be angry? And the answer is no, it was not cruel to be, and yes, I could be angry. I told them as much, and they were in tears, both horrified and baffled by how they'd treated me, a response I can tell you my dad has never remotely displayed with any of us. It doesn't erase what they did, and they know that, and though the wounds all feel the same, I know they are not.

I know this is why most people who have similarly conflicted relationships with their family members will smooth the paper when they speak of them. They will tell you they're close with their family, they love them so much, so perfect, so great. And then, just maybe, if you get them alone on a certain day, they'll tell you they always felt alone, still feel alone, their family wasn't great. And the very next day they might deny this, to you and everyone else. And if you do this, I want you to know I know why you do it. Particularly if one of your family members was just evil, and the rest were . . . complicated. Because you know there is so much goodness in some of your family members and some days, years, lifetimes, it's easier to forgive the deep pain they've caused you, when you know that humanity and compassion lives within them, and why, FUCKING WHY couldn't they have shown it to you sooner? And the answer might be that someone else in your family had tied their hands behind their back and they couldn't. And it will only make you feel worse. Ah, what could've been.

———————

I recently went to the gynecologist for my annual vagina exam. I would truly rather do anything than go to the doctor for so many reasons, not the least of which is the "oh shit, here comes a nervous breakdown in the basement of an office building" forms you have to fill out. These seemingly straightforward forms lay bare everything I carry with me about myself, all of the information that tells a story no one wants to read. And this process always starts off with two words followed by a blank space you're supposed to know what to do with: *Emergency contact:* _____.

Until very recently, this simple question has made me cry in the waiting room of every doctor's office I've ever been in. Because it makes me feel as I have always felt, very deeply: that I belong to no one.

It's not that I don't have people in my life. I have my agents (ha-haha, I listed them first, which is just the loneliest thing), but they aren't obligated to give a shit about me really, beyond business, even though that model seems so cruel to me. I truly assume on some level that with anyone I regularly, truly interact with on any level, it's personal. I don't expect people who see me passively to, I suppose, but I would just assume that if you talk to me almost daily, you should care if I died. If you deal with suicidal ideation or depression or anxiety, that's often part of how you define someone's ability to be close to you, or to be a true friend.

I have some waiting-room friends, my term for people whom I'm in the process of evaluating to see if they're trustworthy, as well as people who've already been through that process but have proven unsafe at various points, which means I'm still trying to determine their long-term eligibility for the role of my friend. (God, even reading that exhausts me; no wonder the idea of getting close to people makes me sleepy.)

People who know me might be tempted to be, like, "This bitch talks about being alone, but there are, like, thirty people in her phone," but here's why my brain feels like that's nothing. Every single one of those people falls into one of the following categories, except for my therapist, who is so great that I recently described her to someone as "my only friend," and this was the saddest fucking thing ever. Still, I have spent most of my life not having a therapist at all, so I'm so grateful I have one now. Anyway, back to the categories:

- I don't know them well enough to tell them when things are really bad.

- They've told me to reach out when things are really bad, and then I've told them when things are really bad, and they didn't write back, and it gutted me.

- They've told me to reach out, reply when I reach out, but don't really seem to have the empathy, bandwidth, or know-how to respond in a way that feels comforting to me, so I don't do it anymore.

- They're selectively helpful, so every time I reach out, I never know if I'll be helped or disappointed, and it feels easier to just stop trying.

- They're super helpful, but I feel like there's an unspoken time limit in terms of how much I can talk about how hard things are, so I usually keep it to about three texts and then change the subject back to them and how I can help them through their day, and they don't challenge me when I do this, and it feels awful.

- They've been really, really wonderful and helpful before, but I don't want to "bother them" again by reaching out another time.

- Work contacts.

- People who are fighting their own gigantic battles and are therefore either too triggering or send me into a spiral where I focus all the energy I should be using on myself to help them survive. With these people, I always leave the conversation feeling used and drained. To be fair, they did not ask me to turn myself inside out to help them, but my brain is so hardwired to kill myself to let someone else live, someone who is actually not dying at all, and give them the blood I need to survive when they've at no point suggested they needed so much as a drop, that I pour mine out into their veins, and since they absolutely did not need it, it overflows, dripping onto the floor, helping no one.

Because of this, I have always obsessively deleted people in my phone as a way to try and protect myself. "Ugh, I just texted Megan that I really needed her because things are really bad, and she didn't reply. Lane, come on, she never replies! She says to ask if you need anything and then she doesn't write back when you do! Delete her number so you don't forget this again!" And then later I'll need that number for something and I won't have it and it's a whole thing, but in the end, that's something I'm willing to deal with. Because it's far better than needing help so desperately, telling myself maybe it'll be different this time, only to be hurt again because of course it won't be.

I have a lot of internet friends with whom I trade voice memos and GIFs, and strangers on the internet who DM me the sweetest fucking things, but on a deep, unrelenting level, I do not have anyone I would call if I were dying. I would blank. I have blanked.

There are people who say things like, "I'm here if you need me, I love you," and I have no idea what the fuck they're talking about, because I don't believe it. Because the people who've said that to me before later turned out to be unsafe. So now when I hear it, my brain thinks, "Fuck this, I'm out," as a knee-jerk reflex designed to keep me safe. It's like my brain says, "Hmm, I'm not sure if there's arsenic in this lemonade, but since there could be, there is. Don't drink it." So I don't drink it. And it might've been wonderful lemonade. Or it could've killed me. But better safe than sorry.

At this point in my life, I often fear it's too late, as if there were a sign-up deadline for intimacy and friends and family and I just kept missing it. And it's not that I want to, but it's so easy to get wrapped up in "But this is the normal time to have *xyz* thing. I do not have *xyz* thing yet. So it is too late for *xyz* thing." Even though my rational brain thinks that's garbage nonsense.

But back to the gyno. The fluorescent lights in the waiting room put pressure on me to hurry up so I can get into the actual doctor's office and get the fuck out of here, so I refocus and hold my pen in a way that means business. Usually I just leave the emergency contact field blank, TBD, we'll see, fingers crossed, I'm fine, maybe they won't notice. But they always do, damn those properly trained, thorough medical administrators. "You didn't fill out the emergency contact," the woman at the front desk said while pointing her pen directly at the violation. "I don't have one," I said, my face turning red. "You can just put down a family member," she said, a little more slowly this time, as though maybe there was a language barrier between us. "I don't have any," I replied, getting angrier, tears mixing with my rage. "Then just put down the name of a friend who would come pick you up if anything happened," she said, inching dangerously close to pity as she saw the tears pool in my eyes. On other occasions I have put down a friend I used to be close to years ago who lives three thousand miles away but would at least pick up the phone, or my roommate, who technically knows me.

In this particular situation I was getting a full exam, STD testing and all, which is really fun if you like looking back at your sexual history for the last year—the highs and lows, the mistakes, the people you used to be able to count on but can't anymore. While readying the HIV test, she asked me, in a tone that suggested she said this twelve hundred times a day, like customs officers who stamp a hundred passports without looking at them, "Do you have a support system should your test come back positive?" My first thought was "Oh, definitely not." And then I panicked about how I suddenly was very, very fucking sure I had HIV. Like, more sure than anything ever. Did it matter that I'd had only one sexual encounter all year? NOT AT ALL. Jesus, those are some fucking scary questions to pose, even hypothetically.

Later, in the exam room, the totally badass, give-no-fucks gyno asked me about my sexual history, and when I told her that the one person I'd been with all year became violent, she asked if I'd reported it.

My reply was "Please," in the way that only someone who knows what happens when you do that does. She followed this with "Have you told your friends?" and I said, while barely letting her finish her question, "Yes, and they don't care." I took a frantic breath before thinking, *Make a joke so she knows you know that's fucked up, but feels like you're fine. TELL HER YOU'RE FINE.* So I added, "They're really cool people." And she said, "Right, well, what about your family?" Jesus, enough with the third degree!!! Just accept that I'm a Cool Girl in a leather jacket who comes from nowhere and is fun and so alluring and shit. Don't look closer and don't make me look closer either. Instead I said, with a quickening pulse and flushed face, "I don't have any family" for the second time that day. And she said, "Well, we're happy to be your support system." I scoffed like I didn't care, but I cared.

On some level I walk through the world like an adult human version of the baby bird in *Are You My Mother?* subconsciously waiting for someone to see that I'm very take-care-of-able, can I live with you now? I know you're my age, but have you ever thought of adopting an adult? It's cool and fun! And I know that sounds stupidly heartbreaking, and I'm not pretending it's adorable and cool, but I know it's there, below the surface.

It's hard not to throw everything I've written so far out the fucking window right now because I don't want you to know this, because I don't want you to hate me for being so sad and not normal, but then I think, What if you know exactly what I mean?

What if you, like me, would at times throw your whole life out the window and walk away, in hopes there was somewhere you could go and buy an entirely new life with new problems, new people, new everything, as if you were replacing a shitty sweater you'd worn through? Except you get only one sweater for your whole life, and anything can happen—theft, weather, cars that splash you with dirt, stains that do and don't come out—but you can't trade it in or take it off. It's just yours and it's you, forever and ever and ever.

So what do you do? Well, as far as I can tell, you explain how your sweater got like this. Why it looks the way it does. And why you put patches where you did, to hold it together and make it look intentional. And you hope people will understand the parts you can't hide anymore, even if you tried.

PLEASE JUST BE A GOOD PERSON SO I CAN FINALLY BE SOMEONE WHO HAS FRIENDS

"Marilla," she demanded presently, "do you think
that I shall ever have a bosom friend in Avonlea?"
"A—a what kind of friend?"
"A bosom friend—an intimate friend, you know—a really
kindred spirit to whom I can confide my innermost
soul. I've dreamed of meeting her all my life."

—L. M. MONTGOMERY, *ANNE OF GREEN GABLES*

When you don't have the affection and/or attachment you should
have at home, it's totally natural that you'd quickly become someone
who is OBSESSED WITH FRIENDSHIPS. Kids with stable home
lives can Make Friends™ in that casual, take 'em or leave 'em way, but
you, poor you, will want to MAKE FRIENDS!!!!!!!!!!!! in a desperate,
gasping for air while drowning kind of way. And so did I.

Because of that, I can say with some certainty that I was bananas
in love with every best girlfriend I ever had from the ages of six to

seventeen. The only reason the to-the-ends-of-the-earth love stops there is because that type of girlfriendship can be harder to come by as you get older. And even when you do find that person, being friends with your very own Rayanne Graff from *My So-Called Life* is not always fun and light and drawing yin-and-yang symbols on your notebooks and shaving your vulvas together. (Though, to be honest, I never watched that show growing up and only got into it a few years ago, despite a guy I knew in my teens telling me I was "such a Rayanne" because I almost—accidentally!!!—hit some nuns with my car when I turned too far to the right in the grocery store parking lot and I am sorry for it every day, poor nuns.)

Very often, best girlfriendship, especially of the middle and high school variety, is more along the lines of near-death experiences and sleeping-with-Jordan-Catalano betrayal. (I think I need to rewatch this, though, because I remember very little about this show except that Angela had, like, zero problems and the show focused on her as though she had ALL THE PROBLEMS. That said, this has been true of eight million shows about men who also have zero problems who feel like they have ALL THE PROBLEMS, so okay, fine.)

For those of you who have yet to experience the awkward teenage magic found within virtually any episode of *My So-Called Life*, Rayanne Graff is the enigmatic, Janis Joplin–esque best friend of straitlaced-until-she-dyed-her-hair-red Angela Chase, and Jordan Catalano was a boy who would fit snugly into any bad-boy-the-teen-girl-has-a-crush-on category in which you'd like to place him. Especially if that category includes qualities like "white guy in a band" and "secretly illiterate."

I was not a Rayanne in high school, but I don't think I was an Angela either. No one is really a fictional character down to a T, but I definitely followed more than led, adored more than was adored.

In other words, my best girlfriend growing up was always some loud, endlessly hilarious, total knockout girl in a crop top and hot pants, whom I stood beside making jokes while covered in glitter and non-threatening supportive cuteness.

In junior high, that girl was Sam. Sam had long blond Court-ney Love hair and shopped at the cool-girl stores in the mall because that was her style, unlike me, who in those years just shopped in the stores that carried the right clothes to avoid bullying. I'm pretty sure "LOOK I'M WEARING ABERCROMBIE EVEN THOUGH IT'S OVERPRICED NONSENSE TRASH PLEASE DON'T HURT ME" was the store's unofficial slogan.

Sam was also an amazing photographer and indulged my love of creating filthy flip-books about a character named Fred who was constantly doing inappropriate sexual things in a hilariously irrever-ent manner, and fake newspapers that were basically a rip-off of *The Onion*, but based on people we knew, because I'd never read *The Onion*. (Which is tremendous foreshadowing, because, years later, it would become my dream to work there—and a dream I would realize.)

If I wanted to spend the whole day speaking in what were prob-ably regionally inaccurate accents, she would too. If I wanted to act out imagined scenes between Ginger and Baby Spice—who I believed had a vaguely sexual relationship—she went there with me. (Obvi-ously I was Ginger Spice. I think that's clear. Also, this was definitely a convenient way for us to be like "We like each other . . . haha, no we don't! Ginger and Baby Spice do! We aren't gay, THEY'RE gay! We're just playing gay CHARACTERS who do gay things, but we don't because we're NOT GAY. Hahaha. If you shout it, it becomes more true!!!")

Sam was the best sidekick ever, though I always felt like *her* sidekick—her weird, goofy friend who would do any dare "as long as it's not physically dangerous or sexual." We had mostly the same taste in movies and consumed them voraciously while quoting all the lines and doing the dance numbers (if there were dance numbers) together and imagining which of the characters we'd most be like when we got older. We'd dream of moving to Los Angeles together, like Romy and Michele, getting an apartment together, and finally, finally being pretty. Granted, I already thought Sam was the hands-down prettiest girl in the world. But not in the way you're picturing her.

Sam wasn't movie-star hot or even the most popular girl in school. But to me, if I can sound like a gayer version of *Love Actually* for a moment, she was perfect. Sam looked like she would've been more at home in the seventies than in the present day, and was also a size 4, and I know this because she constantly talked about how that was too fat. I was twice her size, so I would just stare at her, hoping my confusion would penetrate her like a visual blood transfusion. But that's the thing about teenage girls: Whether you're the heaviest or the thinnest, the most striking or the most plain, the world has effectively convinced you you're hideous. So, uh, you have that in common, though you won't know that until years later.

I'm struggling to describe Sam to you in a way you can see clearly. And not just because I hate lengthy descriptions ("the bookshelf was a soft oak, with big bookends that looked like mountains hovering around trees that had been kissed with snow"—ugh, it's a bookshelf, I get it!!!), but because when I remember people I've really loved, I just remember a feeling. But nonetheless, fuck it. Let's try. You know the quiet girl in your eighth-grade class who kind of scared you, but then occasionally would laugh in a way where it seemed like even she was surprised she had that much joy inside her, and even more surprised it found a way to escape? That was Sam. You know, the girl who was carrying more pain than you realized at the time, but whenever you went left, she went left with you because going left seemed fun? And if you decided to go right while walking like a toad because *that* just seems fun, she was already immediately walking like an A-plus toad and was five steps ahead of you? That was Sam. You know the girl who was the best at every subject because she genuinely cared about school (?), but would also participate in your endless inside jokes about masturbation, AND spit her milk out while you did spot-on impressions of Jewel? That was Sam.

Sam was just game for any weird stuff I wanted to do. I had this computer game in which you could pick out characters and have them act out scenes, and I'd use it to create full musicals. We'd voice all the characters and I'd write parody songs for each of them to sing, and they were honestly the most disturbing musicals thirteen-year-old girls could possibly write. They dealt heavily with "jokes" about child abuse, but every time I think back on them, they were also really fucking funny and I wish I could watch them now, though I can in my head and that's so nice.

One time Sam and I both decided to shave our vulvas on the same night with shitty razors, and we absolutely went against the grain, which you should never do, but we did. And the next day she came up to me in the hallway and said, with uncharacteristic self-consciousness, "Hey," and I said with matched hesitance, "Hey," and she paused for a moment before saying with a laugh, "IT FUCK-ING ITCHES!" And I laughed and said, "I KNOW!!!" And we both vowed to never do that again, though obviously we did.

She was family in the only way I knew it. She made me feel like I belonged somewhere, to someone. We talked all day every day, from the minute we got to school and unlocked our lockers until we walked to the bus together after school. I wished, more than any-thing, that I lived in her house and could go home with her. When

I'd get to my house, we'd immediately call each other and talk until someone made us stop, and then we'd start the whole thing over again in the morning at school.

We used to call the local radio station and request the Divinyls's "I Touch Myself" at midnight and lose our shit when it came on. Everything about it was awesome, from calling in and requesting the song, to the moment when they actually played it, to jumping up and down on the bed and losing our shit while singing along because we genuinely loved the song. My favorite part was when the lead singer would say, "I fuck a sink, just how much I adore you." It would be years, and many karaoke nights, before I would realize she was singing, "A fool could see just how much I adore you," but I still sing it my way because it's way better.

Sam's family wasn't perfect, and as we got older, I found out just how far from perfect it was. Her mom was kind of half there, a reluctant adult who was frequently stern in a way that made it seem like she was reminding herself to be stern in case anyone asked, just so she could say, "I did it!!!" Far as I could tell, she was a woman in her thirties who wasn't sure how she'd gotten to be in her thirties with four kids, but she had, and she seemed very unhappy about it.

Her dad was mostly absent. He had bizarre, and in retrospect almost costume-like, facial hair, like he was auditioning for a Jeff Foxworthy sketch. He always seemed like he hated being married with kids, kind of like a redneck Don Draper. Sam's three brothers were basically dirtier male versions of her, with dandruff-laden bowl cuts and a lot of Nine Inch Nails T-shirts. I one thousand percent would've made out with any of them if given the chance, despite how effortlessly annoying they all were in that specific "dirty-nailed little brother who loves skateboarding and probably upsetting porn" way. If I met them now, I would probably punch them in the face.

Sam's house was a winding farmhouse out in the country that seemed full of magic to me, mostly because she lived there. It was filled with stained glass and had a beautiful kitchen that seemed straight out of an old-timey cottage—full of plants and wooden spoons and marble countertops, with stones lining the backsplash and . . . I'll stop now because I sound like a lesbian real estate agent (whom I'd totally hire). In some ways, I remember her house more than mine. I focused on the details of her house more because I felt safe there, and even now, I can feel what it felt like to be there: like an interloper who always knew she'd have to go home and was trying to memorize everything so she could dream about it when she left.

I sometimes wonder if my imagination is so intense because I spent so much of my life imagining this was not my reality. So it won't surprise you at all to know that I was obsessed with witches as a kid. Obsessed. I grew up heavily influenced by the late nineties, which was basically one giant cauldron filled with black lace chokers and covers of the Smiths's song "How Soon Is Now?" You had *The Craft*, which was seminal, then you had *Charmed* (aka Wiccan house porn), and honestly, that was enough for me. You also had *Practical Magic*, aka one of the best movies of all time, even though it falls apart in the second act when it stops being about two sets of incredible witch sisters and starts being about some moony-eyed doof in a cowboy hat WHO WAS NOT GOOD ENOUGH FOR SALLY OWENS AT ALL!!! and some bizarre attempts at special effects. More than anything at the time (and fuck it, this applies to now too) I wanted a group of women who were all crazy powerful to come over to my house and make lightning appear in my basement while we summoned whomever for whatever reason.

And I kind of got this to happen.

Obviously, Sam was one of the Chosen who would perform a

ritual ceremony in my friend Margot's creepy uncle's apartment in a shitty part of town on Halloween (aka the best day of the year). His apartment wasn't even cool-creepy—it was just a shitty studio that had a weird kitchen—but it was creepy enough.

My costume that year was set to be epic. I was going to be a Rollerblading Fairuza Balk from *The Craft*. I would do crazy eye makeup and wear some sort of witchy velvet top, a very short skirt, fishnets, and Rollerblades. I loved my Rollerblades so much. Not to brag, but I was really, really good at Rollerblading (a by-product of spending as much time outside my house as possible), except for the fact that I never learned how to use the brakes. I couldn't figure it out. I didn't trust them. When I wanted to stop, I would just try to veer off toward a tree or a streetlamp and wrap my arms around it casually—no big deal, I meant to do that. Or I would point my toes into a triangle until I wobbled to a halt. Arguably, way cooler than brakes. [*Shakes head no.*]

At the lunch table one afternoon, I found a way to bring up the idea of the ritual. "Hey, would you guys wanna do, like, a Wiccan ritual the night of Halloween?" My friends stared at me and laughed, thinking I was joking, but I could not have been more serious. I had done research for months. I knew what kind of tools we needed. I knew that sometimes dudes were invited, but that would NOT be the case with me. (According to my references, men got naked, and I was not interested in seeing that, because I loved Halloween and nothing ruins Halloween faster than a male Wiccan's penis.)

I let them laugh for a few minutes and go back to eating their Farmer Bartholomew cookies (I think whoever that person was, he sponsored my school, because all we ate for like six years were these grease-laden cookies that looked like hardened lumps of butter but were DELICIOUS) before I added, "No, but really. We could call the corners and light candles and play cool music." Still nothing. Silence. "Also, we could do an offering to the gods, which means we get to eat pound cake." They were on board.

On the evening of Halloween, I went to Margot's uncle's shit-brick apartment and began setting up in the living room for what would later unfold. Candles over here, incense over there, and "here's all the cake I brought I hope it's enough is one cake per person enough?" in the center. There was truly a lot of cake.

We went trick-or-treating first. I got the most candy in the quickest amount of time because I was on Rollerblades and KILLING IT. But sometimes I'd slow down to talk to Sam. By this time, I'd realized that she was less a best friend and more a "haha wouldn't it be funny if we were gay but seriously I'm in love with you if you wanna get married, hit me up" best friend. She was the family I'd never had before and wanted more than anything, so I treated her accordingly by hoarding and giving her extras of her favorite candies.

"Come on, you guys, be serious!" I barked at them, in as much of a bark as I could muster while also giggling, because I was physically incapable of being serious, because my entire identity had become an airplane with a banner attached that read "HAHA SAD? I'M NOT SAD I KEEP MAKING JOKES WHICH MEANS I'M FINE" that won't stop flying over your house. Plus, Sam was holding my hand in the circle and I was going to marry her for sure.

In my experience, most queer women—and heterosexual women, for that matter, because women absolutely have crushes on guys who don't see them that way—don't get as pissy as some heterosexual dudes get about the Friend Zone. The Friend Zone, while not always ideal, is still a goddamn gift, and really, the definition of true love. If you love someone, or even just care about them, as you claim to, you don't mind the Friend Zone at all, because sure, fine, you don't get to French them and stuff, but you get to know them and be close to them and hear all the dumb things that run through their minds and all the brilliant things that they don't even know are brilliant. You get to know them and share the same air, and you're alive at the same time, which is a gift in and of itself. If you don't want the Friend Zone, you don't want the girl. Simple as that.

Queer women will gladly remain there as long as it takes, whether that means, "As long as it takes for them to realize I'm the one for them, probably," or if it just means, "Okay, they don't think I'm the one for them, so I guess I'm not, and that's okay because they're still wonderful and I will just find someone else."

I always hated when the guys I grew up with would tell girls they didn't "get it" when they'd collectively objectify women and we'd ask them what the fuck their problem was. Or they'd tell us we have "no idea what it's like" to be crazy about a cute girl, especially when she doesn't know you exist or just sees you as a friend. First of all, bro, not everyone's straight. I could totally fathom being crazy about a cute girl, except they're never just cute girls, not ever. They're *everything*, and probably a lot of things those guys couldn't see, or didn't care to see. Plus, hahaha, you think queer women don't know what it's like to be into a girl who just sees you as a friend? Dude, try being into a girl who doesn't even see your gender as a socially sanctioned option!

A straight high school—or even junior high school—boy will never come close to knowing that level of "I don't have a shot with this girl" pain. First of all, you do have a shot, because as far as you know, she's straight or has been told to act straight. Second of all, all our lives, girls are told in not so many words that our main job in life is to please men, don't embarrass them, don't make them angry, give them what they ask for, be nice. So really, men technically "have a shot" with literally every woman they see, because we've all been trained to give you one, or else we're assholes.

We've all been taught to lose our fucking shit if a boy, any boy, has chosen us. "WE HAVE BEEN CHOSEN!!! And now, we must do whatever he wants because it is so special that he has chosen us!!!" It's truly upsetting how persistently that message is communicated to us and how we accept it blindly, on a molecular level. Not attracted to this guy at all? BUT HE CHOSE YOU! Don't think he's funny or kind? STOP BEING SO PICKY, HE CHOSE YOU! Wish he treated you differently? OMG, NO ONE'S PERFECT, AND HE CHOSE YOU! YOU KNOW, ONE DAY BOYS WILL STOP CHOOSING YOU ALTOGETHER IF YOU DON'T CONSTANTLY DATE EVERY GUY WHO CHOOSES YOU AND THEN YOU'LL DIE ALONE, SO FUCKING LET HIM CHOOSE YOU!!! YOU ARE A TEDDY BEAR PULLED OUT OF A SHITTY ARCADE MACHINE AND HE PAID SEVENTY-FIVE CENTS. HE'S YOURS NOW. But with men, in the broadest sense, they get to choose who they do or don't want, like a king deciding which of the seven types of lamb placed before him is suitable for dinner. Mostly because no one cares when men get married, and if they wait until they're forty or fifty or sixty we all assume it's because they haven't found anyone good enough for the high standards we allow them to have for themselves. And then we sneer when women do the same.

Please know that I am not suggesting men put these ideas in their own heads. I truly assume anyone reading this right now is a good person with great intentions who would gladly remove this shitty programming from their own head and the heads of everyone around them who also wanted it gone. God, I wish we could all—every person, regardless of gender—point to the movies or TV or commercials or people who gave us the damaging ideas about what our gender means and what other genders mean, but it often seems like a mixture of sources we can't quite place, making us feel crazy or like we chose to believe this—but ask around, and you'll find we did not.

Back to the ritual. I had to regretfully drop Sam's hand so I could hold the stupid Wiccan book that I wished I'd given enough of a shit to memorize, and let me tell you, if I'd known I would've ended up holding hands with Sam and would've had to drop that hand to read, "Sage the area in a clockwise motion three times," I would've memorized every word and volume of future and past editions to the letter.

As I read it, I realized this ritual was kind of slapped together. We didn't have everything we needed, like a scrying mirror or a coven leader, though I guess that was supposed to be me? Plus, I seriously could not get those girls to focus. They were all over the place, laughing and talking about non-witch stuff. It was a disgrace. A disgrace! So finally I just gave up and ate a ton of cake in the corner alone while "I Want It That Way" played from someone's stereo.

I'd really wanted this to be something. I don't know what exactly. But I wanted what they had in the movies. I wanted friendships that meant something, connections that went beyond making pizza bagels and listening to PJ Harvey. The closest thing I got was when Sam slept over at my house that night. Both of us exhausted, we flopped onto my bed. I don't know how, but we started talking about things that scared us. It wasn't framed that way, but that's what it was, and often is with friends at that age. The gentle and very quiet opening-up that happens late at night when you should be asleep already. You feel safe enough, and maybe sleep-drunk enough, to say the things you can never say when you're wide awake and it's morning, because if you say something you might need to take back, you have a cover.

"Did I say that? Ha, I was half awake last night." Being sleepy is the
being drunk of being thirteen.

She told me, in words separated by pauses, and then sped through
like she was trying to get out all the words before she lost her nerve,
about her cousin and how he used to "make her do things to him,"
and how he'd give her presents at the end. My eyes widened for so
many reasons. She had a family. They were weird, but she had one.
Her mom made breakfast and cared enough to be stern sometimes.
And far as I knew, Sam didn't live in fear of her family, and they paid
attention to her and seemed to give her what she needed. Compared
to me, she appeared to have everything I didn't have. But apparently
she had more of what I had than I knew, more of what I had than
I'd wanted for either of us. And she just cried. For a really long time.
And I cried too, for reasons I couldn't tell her, and because she was
another person I couldn't save, couldn't protect, and why was no one
protecting us? Why? We were kids and someone was supposed to
protect us.

So I held her hand. And I didn't stop holding her hand. So much
so that I didn't even get up to take out my contacts, because I didn't
want to leave her there. I woke up the next morning and my eyes
wouldn't open; they were sealed shut, red and burning. Sam's mom
came to pick her up and I couldn't even see her as she left, except
maybe a little bit through a hot red space in my right eye. I told her
I'd call her tomorrow, like I always did, like everything would be like
it always had been.

This is a time period I live in constantly inside my head, in moments like this, but better. This wasn't Sam giving up on photography
and joining forces with people we'd previously agreed we hated to
bully me in the hallways—both seemingly aftershocks from the end
of our friendship, shaking us both so hard that our lives shattered, in

their own ways, leaving us with no choice but to build entirely new ones without each other.

We went from spending every waking moment missing each other, every evening on the phone, and every weekend at each other's houses, to Sam's completely ending all contact with me; a type of heartbreak from which I don't know if you ever really recover.

I saw her slipping away from me as we got closer and closer, as our jokes about being "gay" became more frequent, and then immediately less frequent, until I was the only one keeping up the jokes, as she'd swiftly change the subject. She started hanging out with a girl named Helen whom we both hated because she was super mean and smelled like a hamster cage. I got us tickets to see Joni Mitchell for my birthday, even though at that time Joni Mitchell was more Sam's favorite than mine, so I had literally gotten us a birthday present for her, on my birthday, which speaks volumes about what I thought true romantic love was back then: all about the other person and nothing about me at all. Healthy stuff.

This whole period of time felt like one long Sunday night, or better yet, Saturday night. I don't know what it is about Saturday night that makes me want to leap off tall buildings in a single bound. I think it's probably because Saturday nights are like weekly New Year's Eves. You're supposed to not be alone, you're supposed to do something So Fun!!! You're supposed to have friends and it's supposed to be the Best, and when it's anything less, you just feel like you're six thousand miles away from your best life, and fun, and normalcy.

She asked if Helen could come with us. I was stunned. Her friend-mistress whom we had both literally hated, like, two weeks ago? "I don't know, she's kind of nice," she said. I retreated immediately. "Well, if you really want her to come, that's fine. I don't care. I just want you there and me there and it'll be great." But something still wasn't right in her voice and I didn't know what. She was silent for a while, and then she said we were getting "too close," she needed to be friends with "other people besides you."

"Okay! That's fine!" I said. But it didn't do any good. She was gone.

I can't pinpoint why she ended our friendship, but I do have theories. For one, I think our friendship blurred a lot of heteronormative lines, and from stories I've heard from other women, this happens a lot. It doesn't even necessarily mean either one of you is queer, but when you're a teenager, there is an overall pressure to be "normal," and spending that much time with someone of the same sex can quickly call "normal" into question. This type of intimacy and closeness is not often socially sanctioned, as we're told it's reserved for your romantic partner, who—in your teen years especially—is "supposed" to be someone of the opposite sex.

We did joke about it. "What if we were gay?" And the more we played house and "joked" about these things, the more I think it started to hit closer to the truth than either of us knew what to do with. So she did something about it.

And then, in true *Heavenly Creatures* minus the murder fashion, her parents moved them somewhere far away and that was that.

I can't say for certain whether or not our relationship was romantic (jk it so was), and really, that's not the point. Either way, I think she also had a very difficult time recovering from what happened between us. I see the effects of this type of thing in women in their twenties and beyond: recovering from finally finding the girl who'll make collages of 1960s starlets for them and cry with them until four a.m. while they tell each other things they can't tell anyone else. But invariably it all gets ruined because one betrays the other, one of them falls in love with the other, or both of them fall in love with each other—and they're too terrified of what people would think about that.

With Sam, she proved my worst fears to be true: that I was too much and needed too much. I've spent so many of my relationships being terrified the person I love will hurt me, and always questioning whether or not the other person really means what they say, and worrying if I love more, or feel more, and what that means if it's true.

The only way I can explain this is by telling you a story from when I was really little. My parents were going out to dinner when I was six or so, and before they left, I felt instantly desperate and went to the bathroom and grabbed my mom's lipstick and put red dots all over my body and then begged them not to go. "I have chicken pox, you can't leave," I said. I remember they both laughed and laughed and then they left. And I cried and couldn't stop. They laughed at me like I was a wacky child pulling a wacky stunt: kids say the darnedest things, etc. But I think about that night all the time, that little kid desperate for someone to love her, take care of her, spend any time at all with her, make her feel connected to literally anyone or anything, and they just laughed. And left.

Not long after this, I realized the only time anyone would take care of me when I was a kid was when I was sick, when they were forced to (and this fell on my mom, because I don't think my dad literally ever took care of anyone but himself). So I made myself sick all the time, just so she'd spend time with me. And I knew the whole time my mom was doing it, she didn't have it to give. Still, as a kid, you can't rationally think, "My mom is barely able to keep her head above water in her own nightmare. It is not personal that she cannot care for me on top of that." All you absorb is "My mom hates taking care of me, I can feel it, she wishes she could be watching TV or reading a book or talking to a friend," but I didn't care. I just wanted her to take care of me so badly I didn't care that she seemingly didn't want to, or that I'd stayed home sick most of the year, or that I'd developed an ulcer by the age of six from stress—yet another warning sign no one noticed.

Even now when I get sick I often get impossibly depressed because I just want someone to take care of me, like I wanted someone to take care of me then, and no one's coming for either of us.

To counteract this, I take a fuckton of Emergen-C at all times, because if I never get sick, I can never get sad!!!

I always think about that "contact comfort" study they did with rhesus monkeys. Basically they paired one set of monkeys with cloth-covered surrogate mothers and no food, and another set of monkeys with wire-covered surrogate mothers with food. The idea was to see which monkeys thrived more: the ones who had comfort and no food, or food and no comfort. Not that surprisingly to me, the ones who experienced comfort and care, despite not having any food, fared so much better. And I have always identified with the kind-of-dying monkeys who technically had food, but desperately wished they had softness and care too.

I know they used mothers in this study only because they supply milk, but I wish we could talk more about the fathers who technically supply food and nothing else. And then occasionally don't even provide the food, and as was the case with my family, take the mother and lock her in a glass case where she could barely function, let alone reach out to love us, like I believe she wanted to, so there is no one left to turn to. I wholly reject the idea that "Well, if the father fails at being a caretaker, or abandons his family, or is abusive, it's expected, what can you do? Men are like this! But if the mother isn't an ideal caretaker, she's a monster." No, I don't agree. Especially when one monster had a very large part in creating the other.

———————

When Sam and I stopped being friends, I went into a deep depression no one at school could understand and I was made fun of every day for crying about it. But they didn't get it. When you don't have a baseline of love and security and home, and you finally get someone who can seemingly love you and you feel accepted and special and you feel like "Aw, is this home? Finally! I can't wait! This is so great!" and then they kick you out, you feel like you've lost everything. You don't have a foundation, so you look everywhere for one, which means the weight of any one connection is so heavy, so important, so delicate. If you lose it, what else will you have? And it has definitely kept me in a ton of awful friendships and relationships because I'd felt like I had nothing or no one else to fall back on. I'd made my "friends" my family, and you fight for your family, and you don't leave them ever. But they're not your family. And they know that. And you don't.

Every so often I hear adult women say things like "I just get along better with men," or "I can't stand other women," or some variation of one of the two. I want to believe with all my heart that those women still long for the close female friendship they had and then lost, or never had at all. I want to believe that some part of every woman remains a teenage girl who just wants to find an unstoppably kind and inspiring girl to laugh with, someone to be in total awe of. But the combination of the indescribable intimacy of women at that age, when everything seems so fraught, and the walls are changing all around you, the floor sinking and rising, and all you want is to grab on to someone you know will go through it with you, makes it the most challenging and necessary thing to obtain.

And if your family is horrible, and then you go to school and everyone there is horrible too, it can feel like everyone is trying to kill you—physically or emotionally—everywhere you go. So partnering up with someone who sees you and thinks you're special, you're perfect, you're choose-able, and of all the people in the whole world (see: school), they'd choose you every time, seems wise. But then one day they un-choose you, and you feel like you're nothing again. "Well, fuck that. I'm not letting that happen again." And then you become That Girl. "I just get along better with men," and you do it for however long you choose to make yourself believe it. But I don't believe it.

I know too many women, myself included, who however briefly tried this role on and then realized it was bullshit. They were just scarred from their childhood female friendships, and that, coupled with a culture that's constantly trying to get you to see other women as an invisible threat to your getting a man or a job or some similar nonsense, made it easier for them to slip right into a pair of Girls Are Too Much Drama, the jeans for women who secretly hate themselves.

I don't think we ever really stop wanting that, though. Even as a grown woman, I still want to go over to someone's apartment, borrow a pair of their pajama pants (and not feel the deep, deep shame I did as a child when their pants didn't fit me, because it was SO MUCH SHAME), and order Chinese food like real adults. I want to put on Spotify playlists and talk until we pass out and wake up to the quiet hum of whatever we were playing come morning, because we only turned it down and forgot to turn it off. And to shake out our messy hair, content in the knowledge that we belong somewhere and to someone, for however long they'll have us. I've had shades of that now and then, and it's a feeling I admittedly chase. When I'm with friends now, as an adult, I don't want to have polite adult tea and talk about our jobs. I don't want to sit in dress pants while we talk about a *New Yorker* article. Not really.

I want to lie on the couch, cozy in blankets, watching movies, feeling safe enough to pass out and stay the night if we want to. I want to turn English muffins into foundations for pizza bagels at ten p.m., even though they're not as good as bagels and we know it. I want to tell each other things we can't talk about online, or we can't tell our coworkers, and to cry and still be lovable, even if we're in pain sometimes. To break in front of each other, and pick up the pieces together, before making some dumb joke and telling each other we love each other and knowing we're safe to be all of it.

MAYBE SOMEONE ELSE WILL LOVE ME AND THAT WILL FIX EVERYTHING

Love isn't here, love isn't here
But it's somewhere.

—PATTY GRIFFIN, "I DON'T EVER GIVE UP"

There's a specific sort of obsession with love that you're bound to find yourself having once you've realized, on any level, that you don't have a family the way you're supposed to. There's a need in there to be normal, to be wanted, to belong to anyone, anywhere, as soon as humanly possible, that really lends itself to loving super-romantic shit of all kinds. Because okay, sure, it's clear the whole "having family like you're supposed to have a family" thing is off the table for me, BUT oh my God, there's this other thing called a "soul mate" AND THAT PERSON WILL FIX EVERYTHING!!! Phew, thank God. I thought I'd have to live in this abyss forever until I overdosed on pills like a sad movie star, but no! All I have to do is wait until I'm, like, I don't know, eighteen years old max, probably, and I will meet my soul mate and I will be loved and I will belong and I will breathe deeply and feel beautiful and protected and at last I Will Be Fine.

I can honestly say I have spent my entire life searching for romantic love in a way that I thought for a very long time was adorable and that I now see as heartbreakingly sad. I'm sure it's closer to the truth to say it's in between the two, but maybe because I've lived it and know where it comes from, it seems mostly like the latter. That intense *Anne of Green Gables* romanticism, bursting from every cell in my body, came from a similar place in me as it did in Anne: a tragic backstory and a desperate need to belong to someone. Unlike Anne, I never met my magical adoptive family, though to this day I continue to long for it with every heartbeat, like an ancient shelter dog that knows it might not have much time left but maybe someone is coming, maybe they are.

I loved Anne Shirley for all the right reasons. She wasn't the right kind of pretty or the right kind of girl; she was too loud, too messy, too romantic, wanted too much, felt too much, and needed too much.

That combination of excessive romanticism, a love of words and language, making anything sound like poetry and anything look like art, and turning all moments into unforgettable flashbulb movie scenes, coupled with my childhood, resulted in my spending a lot of time outside my house, scribbling in my notebook like Harriet the Spy, and occasionally definitely also pretending I was a spy, while splitting that time by trying to hit every Mariah Carey note it is possible for an eight-year-old to hit while she's sliding down the stairs because I've always loved multitasking.

I know I loved all those fictional characters because I was a wild, inquisitive, messy-haired little creature who asked too many questions and loudly questioned her neglect and abuse, definitely not the agreeable living doll my parents seemingly had in mind when they decided to have a child.

I quickly gravitated toward Matilda, Anne of Green Gables, and Pippi Longstocking—all mouthy, whip-smart heroines too weird for their birth families, or simply on their own for reasons unknown. (Seriously, what the shit was with Pippi's idiot dad? She was not old enough to sail the high seas by herself, how was that not clear to him??? What a dick.) I wrapped myself daily in the idea, subconscious as it was, that one day I'd be seen, understood, and loved. I'd belong somewhere. I had to. There had to be some small place in the world for me, and even if that wasn't the case, I'd make one for myself, by myself, somehow.

But even before the obvious abandonment (which began as emotional, and then resulted in the total absence of my parents, with grocery money left on the table and my buying the groceries and getting obsessed with cooking because SURE, I CAN BE THE PARENT!!! I CAN! I CAN BE THE BEST PARENT!!!), or my subsequent coping strategy of "leave before anyone can leave me" relationship patterns, what I did know, and could articulate at length, was my obsession with the idea of soul mates, romantic love, and destiny.

That's a sort of destructive drug on some level, I'm sure, but I was also born with these ideas in my blood and I know it, because I have a reporter's notebook full of meet-cute stories from when I was a kid.

Just as with my persistent British accent of unknown origins (according to my mom, I had not been exposed to British TV and they seriously had no idea where that actually pretty fucking good accent came from), my belief in love came with me, like a specific kind of Barbie comes with a specific kind of accessories. My Barbie came with too much empathy, a heart as big as every ocean, and a mission to figure out how people find love and why, and how I could one day find it too.

I don't by any means think my purpose on this earth is to simply find my soul mate, and I don't think little-kid me did either, as both she and I know that's reductive and, frankly, sexist, but damn if I didn't come out ready to look as hard as I could anyway.

Before my parents openly split up (they were always separated as far as I was concerned), my dad lived in the basement, which is totally normal for a child to observe, yes, absolutely. So all I knew of relationships as a little kid was "everyone is terrified of Dad, and Mom is very, very quiet, and Dad lives in the basement, and everyone is sad."

At the time, my coping mechanism to counteract the constant hiding from my dad like he was a serial killer who would find me any minute now, I can hear him breathing, etc., involved my grabbing several reporter's notebooks and going door to door in my neighborhood, doing what any other little kid my age was definitely, definitely also doing.

[*Knock, knock.*]
Neighbor: Oh, hello.
Me: Hi! How is your day today?
Neighbor: It's fine, thank you.
Me: Wonderful! Ooh, are you making dinner? What is it you're making?
Neighbor: Well, I'm making steak and some potatoes.
Me: Oh my! [Scribbles on pad.] And what recipe do you use? Is that a family recipe?
Neighbor: No recipe, really. Just kind of make this.
Me: YOU MADE IT UP??? That's so cool!

Neighbor: Thank you.

Me: Is your wife home? I see her in the garden a lot.

Neighbor: Yeah, she's out back right now.

Me: How did you meet each other? How did you know she was
the one? Was it one thing or a lot of little things? How long
have you been together? Take as much time as you need. I
have two pens.

The recipe questions were just my gateway into the real shit, the good shit, I was after. And then they'd tell me.

My imagination, which was primarily reserved for writing, directing, and starring in my own plays, or shooting my weird short films, or singing for hours in my room, became part-time fixated on communicating with my soul mate in my head, because why not? That just sounds fun.

It became a never-failing nighttime activity. I would talk to my soul mate like we were in the same room. I would imagine us having adorable conversations just before falling asleep, and my soul mate helping me through whatever was going on at that time, which was often way too much for one person anyway. And I would imagine the hilarious, stupidly romantic things my soul mate would say to me that would stop me dead in my tracks, overwhelmed and unable to reply with anything but a lump in my throat and a relief that we'd found each other, finally.

That's what everyone was doing at eleven, right? Cool. I thought so.

For me, it was less about imagining a romantic ideal and more about having a receptacle for my thoughts and feelings, and a caretaker who saw me for who I was. My soul mate didn't look like Mark-Paul Gosselaar (though I wrote Mark a fan letter when I was, like, six that was basically just "Hi, Mark. I am a fellow teen. Yes, it's true. I am a teen who is your age as well. As we are both definitely teens, we should date).

My imaginary soul mate didn't look like anyone. He was more of a feeling than anything else. (But if I had to describe him, he was a cute boy with Miss Honey vibes who loved me without sexualizing me.)

I didn't even really date around that time. I was horribly bullied back then for three classic reasons: (1) I had glasses. (2) I'd gained weight, due to my well-meaning but checked-out mom giving me four-hundred-calorie Ensure-type drinks as "snacks" to somewhat address my stress ulcer making me too nervous to ever eat anything. (3) I didn't have the "right" anything. And if one time I *finally* had a shirt everyone else had, please God let this be what gets them off my back, SURPRISE! That was even more of a reason to treat me like shit, because I wasn't cool enough to have it, so I needed to be punished . . . because I had glasses? I don't know. Conversely, if I had a shirt *no one* else had—and if no one else has it, it's clearly lame because fuck individuality, you're in sixth grade, this is fuckin' Thunderdome, BITCH—that too was a great reason to treat me like shit. I am thoroughly convinced most children from eleven to fifteen are garbage monsters from hell because they're all just miserable. I'm able to look back now at my bullies and sigh and go, "Well, I'm sure things weren't great at home and their parents were hateful elitist assholes, but I was already getting treated like shit at home, so, um, if they could've, like, not been abusive to me at school on top of that, that would've been so chill. But you know, love and light and forgiveness and stuff. Except for . . ." (*lists forty-five people who will never escape my wrath*).

It was around this time that I began online dating because, yes, I was the most underage I could possibly be, but also, I had no adult supervision, I was super romantic, and I just wanted to get the fuck out of my house to somewhere safer, somewhere better. You'll be shocked to know that is not what online dating leads to for thirteen-year-olds.

I don't even want to go into what it led to, but let's just say there are a tremendous number of creeps and predators in their early twenties who are actively trying to hook up with thirteen-year-olds, and they did not tell you that shit on *Nightline*. (I don't remember ever telling anyone I was eighteen, though I do remember having to be eighteen to set up a profile, but then, in the interest of transparency, telling guys in the messages that I was not eighteen at all, and literally no one minding.)

Boys at school weren't really an option, as I'd been made to feel that I was so ugly you wouldn't even want to look at me, and I definitely remember spending most of my childhood praying no one would, so I wouldn't get hurt. This is something I never understand when I look at old photos of me, but I guess people get assigned roles at the time and mine was "make fun of her for being hideous and gross," and I bought it. But I still, on some level, felt like maybe, just maybe, someone in some city somewhere would think I was kind of pretty. Like in a different market, maybe? So I met a lot of boys online who were my age who went to neighboring schools and were crazy hot.

My first non-creep boyfriend, Wes, had a six-pack and looked like he would be the lead in any Hollywood movie about hot teens and was unrelentingly sweet and kind and worked with the elderly because he wanted to. But I broke up with him. And I would bet that it was because on some level, I felt like I'd been assigned the wrong one. "He's gorgeous and kind and sweet and in love with me, who is firmly unlovable. My parents don't love me, I'm bullied at home and at school, and you, superhot teen with a SIX-PACK BECAUSE IT'S WORTH SAYING AGAIN, love me? Let me solve this problem for you and break this off."

And so I went back online. Subconsciously, I'm sure, looking for something a little more like what I was used to.

The next guy I met online was also an age-appropriate boy named Sean (which just shows you that there truly were a lot of underage teens looking for love online, so it was technically not just me doing this. Sadly, there were also lots of pedophiles). Sean was super cute and sweet and very tan and had lost his virginity at nine. That depressed me then and depresses me now. At thirteen, he invited me to a party with him where I would, having zero prior experience with drugs or alcohol, casually drink, like, ten beers and fourteen shots of rum, swallow a huge tab of acid, and smoke weed while I watched Sean make out with his ex in front of me. I blacked out shortly afterward, and all I remember of that night was being unable to move or speak on the bathroom floor and vaguely hearing some dude say, "Hey, Sean, your girlfriend is, like, dead or whatever. You should probably take care of her," and his opting to instead finger his ex in an adjacent room.

Now, I think of my tired, overdosed little-kid self, who only wanted someone to love her, no matter what it took—drugs? Okay! Alcohol? Sure!—lying there on the floor alone in a little ball, waiting for anyone to care about her, and all I want to do is pick her up and kiss her forehead and tell her I'm so sorry I couldn't protect her.

I came home late that night (a twenty-nine-year-old who owned the apartment where preteens fucked and drank drove me home) and sang Fiona Apple songs into the mirror and watched my pupils dilate until it was time for school, like nothing had happened.

Having decided that the only reason things didn't work out with

Sean was because he wasn't "mature," I went back online to meet more potential "boyfriends." This time, they were men who were nineteen to twenty-four, and would try to coax me to have sex with them near overpasses, and when I wouldn't, or would cry because this is not how I saw this going at all, they'd get angry. I wish I could go back in time and tell myself, "Lane, you're worth more than this, and also, these guys are pedophiles," but I didn't even recognize these moments as wholly negative situations. When you grow up without real parenting or boundaries, you can talk yourself into believing it's totally normal for twenty-four-year-olds to date thirteen-year-olds.

I very naively, and very genuinely, wanted someone who would make me mix CDs and love me and watch *Empire Records* with me while we ate tacos, and instead I'd end up being driven home by an adult man who'd called me ugly and worthless for refusing to blow him outside a Denny's.

And I'd go home and lock myself in my bathroom and throw myself into work, which at the time was spending seven hours trying to hit every single note that Stevie Nicks, Nina Simone, Sarah McLachlan, Patsy Cline, Gwen Stefani, Debbie Harry, Dinah Washington, Shirley Manson, Shania Twain, the Cranberries, Lauryn Hill, Diana Ross, Selena, Fiona Apple, and Luscious Jackson (who many years later would tell me they loved my voice [!!!] and ask me to play in their band and sing harmonies with their lead singer, Jill Cunniff, on the very songs that kept me going as a kid, which was beyond surreal) could hit. I loved singing the songs in exactly the same way each person sang them, leading me to be able to sing like anyone.

Years later, a friend of mine from school was listening to me sing along to these songs and realized I sounded just like them and was blown away that I could do that, which made me realize, for at least half a second, that maybe that was something special. Not me, no, no, no, but something I could *do*. I'd record audio of *Daria* episodes and *Comedy Central Presents* so I could listen to them at school any free moment I got because it was a lot better than listening to the bullying. Then I'd make some food and go on to phase two, aka watching *Late Night with Conan O'Brien, Upright Citizens Brigade, Strangers with Candy*, maybe a movie, then *Blind Date*, then infomercials. Then I'd sleep for an hour and go to school. And then I'd go back online and try again, because, well, they say dating is a numbers game.

And the thing is, our culture totally reinforces the shit out of the normalcy of these guys. We tell kids that pedophiles are fifty-year-old creeps with candy in vans, and then we also tell them, via episodes of TV and movies, that it is totally normal for fifteen-year-old girls to go out with twenty-one-year-old college guys and that ONLY THE COOLEST, HOTTEST, MOST MATURE GIRLS GET TO DO THIS!!! So, as a very new teen with no parental guidance, I was, like, "Fuck it, I'm like thirteen, let's start dating!" I mean, have you seen *Dawson's Creek* where Pacey sleeps with his teacher? I was told this is hot. Or when Buffy (or literally any underage girl on any show or movie from any era) goes to a college party and the guys are jerks but some of them kind of aren't, and anyway the point is, again, you have been chosen and what a great feeling and also, what is statutory rape?

I don't ever remember being afraid of dating older guys, possibly a by-product of already having survived so much, so what was the worst that could happen? A very, very dangerous question to pose. And even if I was scared, it was worth it to take the shot that one day someone, somewhere, of any age, would love me and want me.

When we see teenage girls in movies who "seduce" older men, we paint them as bad girls in crop tops, bad seeds in purple lipstick, troublemakers with lip rings, jailbait—sexy, sexy little teens with crazy horny brains. What we don't ever talk about is what they're looking for, what they're running from, and why they're running toward any kind of love or attention at a terrifying speed. We don't ever talk about those girls, some of whom might be openly "sexy" looking, and some of whom might just dress like "normal" little girls, who aren't looking for sex at all, and are truly just looking for love, or caretakers, or a place where they're wanted, even if they're looking somewhere those things will never be found.

For me, what I found instead was guys in their twenties who would show me bestiality porn and offer me beers before yelling at me for having "chipped nail polish, what the shit. Next time don't you fucking come over here looking like this." Subconsciously, I know I heard this and thought, "Yes! Sign me up. Abuse! Neglect! Telling me to be whoever you want me to be! Being a sexual object owned by whoever! I know this song, every word! Where's my lighter so I can hold it UP?"

In the breaks between "dating" pedophiles, I focused my attention on the lackluster boys at school. But I do remember thinking one guy was totally cool because he "worked at a hotel washing towels." Good shit.

Alas, Captain Towels and I were not meant to be, in the same way those who came before and after him were not meant to be, because that's just kind of how dating works. You just date a fuckton of Not Meant to Bes until you have one (or however many ones you believe you get to have in life) Meant to Be, and then you collapse into an easy chair, like, "Fucking finally. Can we just eat scones now and make out and have fun and change the world and be cute for the rest of our lives? Finding you was exhausting." And then, I assume, they bring you scones and brush your hair back and kiss your forehead and just say, "Yup."

Talking to my soul mate every night definitely struck me as not normal, but I was never normal to begin with, so if I was going to be weird, I was going to be the kind of weird that made me happy. And this made me happy. Because on some level, I assumed my soul mate was probably doing the same thing. Somewhere in the world— maybe my same country, maybe not—they were talking to me, sharing all their shitty and wonderful stories and what they did that day and what they hoped we'd do one day and saying good night to someone who didn't exist yet, but definitely also did, technically, probably. And it was my favorite part of the day. A nightly meditation on the probability that one day I would find them.

Sometimes I'd wake up with them too, and say good morning, and kiss them, and tell them about the dreams I'd had. Other times I was way too busy and had to get to school. As the years went by and I receded further into my own imagination, I began to talk to them all day and all night long. I would tell them everything I felt for them, everything I hoped for both of us. I would tell them, wherever they were in the world, that if they were having a hard day, I hoped it got better and that I wished I could tell them they were lovely and I saw them and they were special. I would tell them stories about my day, imagine us ending our day together in the same place, laughing and making out a lot. Things like that.

Years later, I remember this tradition taking a more bizarre turn when I would occasionally apologize to this concept of a person when I'd dated someone who was awful to me, and I technically "let them" be awful to me, and I knew my soul mate would not be pleased with that at all. I saw my soul mate as someone who wanted the best for me, someone who wanted me as safe and happy as possible until they could come and make me as much of each as possible themselves. Just as I'd hate the idea of my soul mate being out there with someone treating them like shit. But then I'd remind myself that I'd never be mad at my person for sticking around for that, because I get it.

You do the best you can with what you have and where you came from and all of the overlapping messages there. And because I would know and I could tell them how easy it was to settle for something over nothing, to take on people like broken-down houses you could totally invest a lot of time and money into and make new again, only to find out they were money pits all along. And I would remind them that, no, this is not all they deserved. Not even close.

I can see now that I used the idea of a soul mate to give myself some sort of parental figure, some sort of protector, someone who was able to see that everything that was happening was not okay, that I deserved more, who could validate everything I was experiencing, since no one around me seemed like they'd be doing any of that any time soon. And if that figure didn't exist, I would make one up.

On the one hand, I had some doubts that my soul mate existed because it was so hard to believe anyone that wonderful could exist. It was easy to doubt that all of the odd combinations of very specific things I wanted to exist in one person could in fact do that and that he would also live in my city and be my same age—like, wow, what are the odds on that? Because I doubt they're bankable.

But on the other hand, I knew *I* existed and I figured maybe my soul mate was out there somewhere thinking maybe I didn't exist, but I totally do, so it was only fair that I believe he exists too.

And then one day I met a boy named Adam on a class trip to Germany. He went to my school and was friends with all my friends and was a nerdy skateboarder who wore a lot of hoodies and looked like a young Adam Horovitz from the Beastie Boys. And since I had finally started dressing like the sparkly, blue-haired punk-rock kid I was, instead of a sentient sign that just reads "PLEASE DON'T

HURT ME," we were a perfect match. But we'd never met before the trip. I don't remember much about the beginning of the trip, but I remember being at a restaurant and not loving the food I'd ordered because it was truly gross (sorry, specific German restaurant). I made a joke about this to the group, and he gave me his soup. Even now, this act makes me smile in its simplicity, because that's really what I needed. Some simple, purehearted, age-appropriate thoughtfulness.

We talked and flirted the whole time in the most innocent way possible. I worried that the amount I joked about sex and mastur-bation would terrify him or, worse yet, make him think I was some-one who'd sleep with him super quickly, which LOL, because I had definitely not had sex with anyone and had very firm and unyielding plans to lose my virginity to another virgin who was a Capricorn, for my own complicated, astrologically based reasons. I don't remem-ber his sign and it doesn't matter. What does matter was that I am counting him as the first boy I ever dated because I refuse to count a twenty-four-year-old on a "date" with a thirteen-year-old as a fucking date because it's not, and it's important to note that.

Sexual assault is not your "my first time" story if you don't want it to be. Some creepy age-inappropriate piece of shit driving you to an underpass doesn't have to be your first-date story if you don't want it to be. Count what you want. You can't change what they did, but you can change your landmarks. It's not a rewriting of history. It's a telling of truths and separating abuse from moments that are supposed to be nothing like abuse at all.

And because you can do that, my first kiss was with Adam—something I would never have guessed on that trip to Germany while I was wandering around, hoping to run into him, excited to make him laugh, letting him nervously try to make me laugh too. But I'm sure it would've elated me to know that kiss was in our future.

All the genuine worries I relayed to my friends in a stairwell at the hotel late one night—about Adam's thinking I was "fast" (LOL) and therefore "easy" (it is not currently 1952, but man, you wouldn't know that from this paragraph) because I was constantly making masturbation jokes and drawing R-rated flip-books—that were laughed off by every single one of them. "Okay, sure, you joke about sex a lot, but your jokes are never super dirty, they're just funny!" And I had no reason to worry, because Adam was the most innocent and sweet first boyfriend who was not a sexual predator that I could've had.

When we got back home from the trip, Adam invited me over to his parents' house to watch *Star Wars*, aka our "date," because he was totally That Guy. And to my credit, we watched like five minutes of it and I was, like, "What if we went somewhere else and did . . . not this?" And thank fucking God, we did.

Adam said he was so excited that I wanted to date him, since he'd never dated anyone before, and his parents would be thrilled to know he wasn't gay. I joked that they'd bake him a cake that said, "Yay, Not Gay," and we went to get soft-serve ice cream and skateboard while listening to my punk mix CDs. It was lovely. We had our first kiss on my elementary school playground, though I was in high school at the time. I'm sure I'd suggested we go there because I love playgrounds and I never got to be a child. He told me I was his first kiss, like he was really excited that it got to be with me. And I really, really was too. Unfortunately, Adam and I didn't last very long, because pretty much the second we kissed, he became Too Much.

He called me what felt like forty times a night, to the point where my mom noticed—and given that her parenting style at the time was "I'm never home and if I am my door is locked, I don't live here, you don't exist, please move out, are you eighteen yet, God I hope so, I can't deal with this right now," that says something. He waited for me after every class, which if it hadn't been coupled with the forty calls and messages a night would've been sweet. It was just too much, and I had to end it, which bummed me out, but he was too intense and smothering. Months later, he'd message me and tell me he was really sorry he'd smothered me and was so intense, but he liked me so much and didn't know what to do.

I've seen this pattern play out in my adult relationships too, in a way. I've dated men who were so sweet and kind and wonderful, but moved way too fast, claiming me as their girlfriend after one date, texting me nonstop all day every day, saying "I love you" after a few dates. And once I learned about attachment theory, I knew exactly why I went for it.

Basically, there are three primary attachment styles: secure, avoidant, and anxious, and occasional combinations of avoidant and anxious. Your attachment style develops in childhood via how you attached or didn't attach to your parents, and then often translates to exactly how you do or do not attach to people when you get older. People who have a secure attachment style have no problem attaching to people or getting close to people or exploring relationships, or relying on people; it comes naturally to them because it came naturally to them as kids (or because they've done the work in therapy to get there).

Avoidant people want that closeness but are scared of it, so they tend to be less expressive with their feelings, view themselves as unworthy of a reliable, responsive partner, and often would rather be alone than deal with potential rejection or pain.

And then we have my attachment style, are you excited??? Anxious attachment! Yeah, shout-out to my anxious attachment people! Granted, you and I can never form a close relationship with each other because two of us together is death, but high five, because I know how much this one suuuucks!

These are people who want to be close with people, but feel like other people don't want to be as close as they do (too many feelings). They don't want to be alone, but they also feel like other people don't value them as much as they value people (too many feelinggggs). They need high levels of intimacy, approval, and responsiveness, and often become dependent on the person they're attached to, to the point where they can feel safe only when they're in constant contact with the person they're attached to, and if they don't have that, they will blame themselves (toooo manyyy feelinggggs). Fun, right? Also, this is absolutely me.

What's so fascinating about all this to me is that if you have an anxious attachment, you're pretty much compatible only with secure attachment people. That's it. If I tried to date an avoidant person, they wouldn't want to be with me (or anyone) anyway, and even if they did, they would just be an unreliable mess I could never feel truly safe in, so it makes sense that I spent so many years being attracted to guys who were, like, "Lane, you're it for me. I'm in. It is easy for me to express this and move within it; let's go!" and for me to be, like, "Yay, but also you're kind of a lot. Is there a way to get a secure attachment who isn't smothering? No? Oh, well, I'll take what I can get! At least you're consistent, that's fine, I'll work with it!"

It's better than abuse, but not any healthier. There's a middle ground. I knew there had to be, and this wasn't it. But it did feel great to hear him say, "I was acting in a way that wasn't cool. You should've ended it and I don't blame you."

Adam told me he'd learned a lot about women from me (which I smirked at then and I smirk at now) and was now dating someone else and wanted to thank me. It seemed like a really fucking obnoxious thing to say then, and it seems like an obnoxious thing to say now, but he was a teenage boy, guys, and in retrospect, for a sixteen-year-old boy, that was actually pretty insightful and mature and sweet. So it will not surprise you to know Adam is now very happily married to someone who seems very nice, but whom I have never met because I got this information from the internet.

But the fact that we didn't work out doesn't matter anyway because he was movie previews. And I knew I had my whole life left to have a ton of even better relationships, just a ton of them! That life would just be an endless string of super romantic, super cute boys who were incredibly nice to me and emotionally available, but, like, way more mature—haha. And it would be up to me to choose the best one, whenever that time came. The world had told me I was just a kid and high school relationships are dumb and just practice for bigger, better relationships! And I had all the time left in the world.

NOW YOU GET TO BE AN ADULT, EVEN THOUGH YOU WERE ALWAYS AN ADULT. GOOD LUCK!

When I'm alone I feel a slow-ticking wildness in my mind.
It's late at night and I am blinded with the city lights in my eyes.

—WILD ONES, "DIM THE LIGHTS"

When I was little, we took a trip to New York City and I just remember seeing people walking around, and thinking, "Everyone here looks sad."

I never thought I'd live here, not even for a second, but listen, when you're crying on a bus and the voice of Stevie Nicks pops in your head and tells you, "Move to New York City, everything happens for you there," you go, "Uh, okay. Thanks, Stevie Nicks, who is still very much alive and therefore I guess is transmitting this message to me via the powers of her mind? . . . Okay, sure. Let's move to New York City." And that is absolutely what happened (well, give or take your belief that Stevie Nicks sent me brain messages on a bus).

Throughout my childhood and teen years, I read countless books and articles about how people "made it," and almost all of them boiled down to "Well, my uncle was the voice of Pumbaa in *The Lion King*, so he was already superrich and successful and I crashed on his couch and then yay, fame." (Which I'm sure isn't the actual story of Ryan from *The O.C.*, but in the issue of *Entertainment Weekly* I read, it definitely seemed like it.) I had none of that. I was surrounded by complicated, creative people but didn't have a support system, let alone a series of rich uncles with eight-picture deals at Sony.

The closest I had was my aunt and uncle, who were gospel singers and had actual albums!!!! And this blew my fucking mind. I would stare at their cassettes for hours, dreaming of one day having my own album. I had no idea that they'd just recorded it in church and put it out themselves and gave them out to their friends. I didn't care. It had a real cover and real liner notes and I wanted that in a way I can still feel in every part of my body when I think about it.

I kept looking everywhere for The Way, the one path that would get me to where I wanted to go, but every time I would ask someone for help, I'd get the old "Well, you can't be an actor and a comedian and a writer and a singer and a director—pick one." And I would sigh and say, "But what if I'm meant to do them all?" and they would look at me like I was annoying and I'd go back to my room and watch another eight movies and then lock myself in the bathroom and try to hit another five high notes and attempt to produce pronounced lengthy vocal runs without taking a breath in between, or work on the books I'd write, and would later ask authors who came to our elementary school, "How did you become a writer?" with wonder in my eyes and a sweet exhaustion in theirs that I recognize now. If I met little-kid me now, with her big anime eyes, desperately ready for her adulthood to start because her childhood was killing her, I'd look at her the same way.

When I got to my Brooklyn apartment—that I'd never seen before because it seemed decent enough on Craigslist, although it had zero photos at all, but it was cheapish and they didn't mind that I was having to move in sight unseen (probably because of what was about to happen)—a bunch of hippies on bikes, with dirt on their knees and Manic Panic hair, stared at me as I pulled up in a truck filled with everything I held dear.

One of the hippies (all of whom smelled horrifically) led me into the room, which was instantly terrifying. There were homeless men staying in the "common area" and junkies (who were doing naked yoga) screaming angrily through the halls.

My room had a dirt floor and four walls streaked with urine.

I was given a shelf that looked like someone had been spending some time (and by this I mean maximum three minutes) at Michaels craft store, which would have been fine but you can't put a decoupage vase in a jail cell and call it homey.

The guy who showed me the room said, "So, here's your room! Yay! It's yours and it's fabulous!"

Guys. It's one thing to describe my room as fabulous when I'm miles away from its view. It's a completely different thing to call something that even prison inmates would describe as "gross" as fabulous when I'm watching bugs form a pile in the corner.

It smelled like stale air and had no windows; gnats swarmed around me as I brought in one bag after another.

I kept thinking about families on TV or in movies who would've seen this and screamed, "Hell no! My daughter is NOT staying in this shithole! Let's go." Instead, I told myself I would survive it, it would be fine.

I went back to my room and tried to put my things away; trying to see if this could work, like maybe I'd missed another fifty square feet. Maybe the bugs had gotten bored and left; maybe they were just passing through, or were Disney bugs who sang and could keep me company! Yeah! No.

My bed was soaked through from a sudden rainstorm on the drive and my feet were covered in the filth that permeated every corner of the space.

The artists' collective was appropriately named WTF Real Estate. (I think this was their attempt to be, like, "man, we're really turning New York City real estate on its head and doing our own thing.") Had they thought it through, they would've added, "which, by the way, sucks."

There was a zombie party that night, so I went, mainly to keep from crying. I got dressed up and ate a disgusting dinner with the hippies. I got my zombie makeup done at the party and talked to supremely boring hipsters and watched their ironic dance moves and half-ass attempts at being impressive.

The open loft space was full of more bugs than I'd ever seen inside or outside one space, climbing the walls, no windows, terrifying people from the ages of eighteen to fifty-five squished into the small rooms, each bolted shut with multiple locks. There was also a pile of free (expired) vegan foods salvaged from a dumpster-diving mission and crawling with at least AT LEAST 2,000 ants, so, you know, I had access to . . . that.

My room (I just laughed out loud when I called it a room—okay, okay, okay I'm good) was windowless, with a dirt floor that could hold a queen-size bed and nothing more, save for that lone "I'm having a nervous breakdown from living in this room, so I went to Michaels" shelf with flowers painted on it, left over from the last tenant who maybe died there, I assumed. And as soon as I'd absorbed that information, I was immediately told what I had not been told via email or on the phone, which was that I'd also have a roommate somehow in that tiny, terrifying storage shed full of remnants from a now-ghost who definitely did not haunt the room because I guarantee once she died, she was, like, "Fuuuuck this place."

So I quickly dissociated and headed back into the poorly lit apartment like it was my unfortunately very familiar destiny, muttering to myself, "Just tell yourself it's like *Rent*. Even though you hated that play, just tell yourself it'll be like that."

I attempted to hang out with the other kids who lived there because I was technically super young and cool and maybe I would've thought this was awesome if I hadn't already lived in a bag full of shit for most of my life before this. I'm sure if I was like these kids, who mostly came from rich families and absolutely wanted to spend their early twenties fucking each other in a filthy artists' space with no locks on the doors because even if something happened, so many of them were whole, they had families, they had money, they were fearless, had the privilege of being able to be fearless, I would've loved it. But because I had no safety net, nowhere to go if this didn't work out, $200 in the bank, and a mission in life to fucking survive so I could live to see the day my dreams came true, I did not love it.

I ended up talking to a cute guy (who desperately wanted to be that dude from Interpol) on the roof who seemed like he was happy, so how bad could it be? *Whispers* very bad if you are not a rich kid who thinks this is cute. Literally, this whole house was the lyrical plot of Pulp's "Common People," which I listened to constantly during this time, singing along with the headphones that never left my ears: "Watching roaches climb the wall / If you called your dad he could stop it all."

I'd been surrounded by happy, fail-proof rich kids my whole life. I'd dated them; I'd watched them drive BMWs to high school while I drove a car as old as I was, a car I'd also live in after graduation. And unknowingly, in all of that, I'd spent a lifetime preparing to move to a city fucking full of insanely rich kids who got $100,000 to give it a go and play at being adults. I'd listen to Pulp or whatever else was in my rotation at that time (Julie Doiron's "Goodnight Nobody" and Cat Power's *The Covers Record* were mainstays) while sitting in the corner, staring at these kids who loved being on their own for the first time in a playfully shitty situation they got to navigate like it was the Sims. But for me, it was my millionth time being on my own in some repulsively shitty situation I had to survive and couldn't hit "game end" when I didn't want to do it anymore.

I didn't hate them, I don't hate them. Because that's the life you're supposed to have at that age. Stupid and frantic, and fucking up and getting bailed out and trying again. I've just never known it and I wish I had.

The kids (I was easily the youngest person there, but have literally never felt like the youngest person in any room I've ever been in. Even when I was ten, I was easily forty in trauma years) were all making a huge pot of something in the kitchen and I was just so excited by the mere concept of someone making me dinner at all and hoping maybe it would be a community, a misfit family I'd never had. I ate my tiny bowl of "Honestly, what is this?" that was probably like 99 percent pubes and I felt happy. I met a punk-rock musician girl who was very tall and seemed very kind and I just told myself I belonged somewhere, finally, maybe, eventually, sort of. (Spoiler: After I moved out, I ran into this girl months later at a café. She told me she was raped in that house by her roommate and the manager calmly suggested she "talk it out" with him and refused to get her a new roommate. She eventually ended up living on the street for a while, and I wished so badly that I had enough money to take her with me.)

I went back to my room and shut the door and went to fall asleep on my 1,000 percent still soaking wet mattress. While trying to sleep on the mattress that was so fucking wet, dude, just soaked through, and the place had no windows or air or anything, like a tiny jail cell, so it wasn't drying any time soon, I started crying while heroin dealers banged on my door with four broken locks, ear infection creeping into my left side, piss-stained walls, the smell in my hair for the next six days, no windows, no toilet paper, more bugs on the walls than paint, stacks of dumpstered food ravaged by worms and ants overtaking the tables, empty cigarette cartons now filled with used condoms, and cried myself to sleep.

I woke up the next morning with an ear infection from the mattress, and the only thing that dragged me out of that room was Liv. Liv was a friend I'd met online in the weirdest way possible: through a guy named Dan I'd briefly flirted with on the internet and never met in real life, who one day introduced us over the phone because he thought we'd get along. Fun spoiler: She and I are still friends now, and Dan sucks. We quickly bonded over our love of old movies and Amy Sedaris and vintage clothing and blue water and a lifetime of intense trauma leaving us both with an eternal need to write, make jokes, and steer clear of most people. If Liv hadn't somehow magically broken through her agoraphobic barriers to come see me all the way from Baltimore, I would have stayed in there, in that room, crying crying crying and begging God to make it different.

Though I'd known her a while at this point, it was through the phone only, since we'd never been anywhere near the same city, and she struggled with severe agoraphobia, but this trip made it real. We went to a nearby gay bar and made penis buttons and wore paper sailor hats. We listened to bouncy Britney Spears songs and laughed at the irony of the carefree music that played around our conversation of uncertainty and the inevitability of the nightmare I'd have to walk back to.

Liv tried her best to get me to come back with her to her parents' Baltimore home (which was just as unsafe if not more so, for both her and me) and just leave everything for now, but it all seemed like too much—the bolt in the night. To leave my stuff there that long, or weigh the odds they might notice that I was gone, or what could happen to every single thing I owned over the course of that day. I'd never had that thing of, like, "Leave stuff at your parents' house," because the second I left home, I gave away or threw away everything and I regret it all the time, but I know why I did it. I didn't know if I was ever coming back or could come back, and I didn't want to leave something and later need it and have no way to get it back, or have a way to get it back that was too painful to attempt. So I put on a brave face and walked Liv to the subway and we lied to each other that we'd be okay, because the truth was too sad, and neither of us could set the other free from their lives.

The next day, I tried to make the best of it and address all the things that made me nervous head-on with the apartment manager. He fed me some *The Secret* bullshit about empowering myself enough to *not* feel like this place was dirty and then asked me to cut some green chilis for the community dinner. I almost started singing, "I'm gonna sit at the welcome table / I'm gonna sit at the welcome table one of these days, Hallelujah!" a reference to *Strangers with Candy* no one there would've appreciated.

If you're wondering why I didn't just leave and find another apartment, know that it never crossed my mind once. A combination of being taught from birth to survive anything, I had become a creature who could deny all my physical and emotional needs existed. I don't even feel them anymore; if I can get through it and not die, I have no other needs. A huge part of this, I think, came from my lack of a capital-letter Family, a lack of having backup. I've talked to friends who will say when they've been in shitty situations, they'll call their parents. I truly don't know anyone with family who doesn't use them all the time like a fucking credit card with every dollar matched by cash back rewards. When I've been in dire circumstances, or had a roommate screw me over on a deposit I was owed or a job that just didn't pay me because "Laws? what laws," it was "You're on your own, kid." There was no "Oh, I'll call this person for help or advice." There was only a voice in my head saying, "Fucking figure it out on your own and stop whining. It's not that bad."

After the extremely unhelpful cult speech ended, a strange but very helpful-seeming man who lived there approached me and told me he could "help you figure out food stamps if you want" and advised me to "put three locks on your door. These people are fucking insane."

I'd been through worse, though, so I was fine, I was cool. And I was gonna make this place fucking homey.

I went to grab a communal fan from the living room to put in my windowless room that was so hot it choked you the second you walked in, and soon after, the homeless guy who crashed in the living room snapped the lock off my door and took it back, claiming it was his. He came and went through the front door to the facility, which was never locked and couldn't even lock if it willed itself to.

Terrified, I spoke to the building manager, who responded with "You know, staying here is all about perspective. If you think this place is terrifying and unsafe, then it is."

Realizing that was literally batshit crazypants logic, I quickly found a local hostel just down the street, and made arrangements to move everything I owned, by myself, in the middle of the night to get to safety.

But just because I had a plan does not mean I was out of that shithole yet—oh hell no. That would've been too easy. Fortunately, I hadn't yet given the apartment manager my rent money, since when I asked when it was due, they said, "It's chill, whatever," and I quickly realized nothing about this housing situation was chill and if anything was "whatever," it was their general view on safety and cleanliness. As I waited outside for my taxi to help me carry my stuff down the street, I was harassed by a heroin dealer who yelled at me until I told him my name, and when he asked, "Where the hell do you think you're going?" I told him I didn't have enough space in my room for all my stuff, so I was taking everything else to a friend's house to make space for my floor cot and my surprise roommate in my Bushwick jail cell. A super cute guy in his twenties intuitively knew what I was doing and said, "Hey, let me help you," and I said, "Thank you so much. This is terrifying and I'm worried of what they'll do to me if they know I'm leaving, but I can't stay here." He said, "I get it, man. These people are crazy," and helped me load everything into the cab, and I briefly married him in my mind. I remember seeing some of the other guys in the rearview mirror of the cab, quickly realizing I would not be back and yelling things at my cab as I left, but fuck it, I was gone, I'd made it out, as I thankfully always had.

When I got to the hostel in the middle of the night in the dead, sweltering heat, with all my stuff in tow, I was told the elevator wasn't working and that I would be staying on the fourth floor, which meant that at three a.m. in 98-degree weather, in a building with no air conditioning, I would be moving everything I owned up about four flights of stairs by myself. I told my story about the apartment full of drug dealers to the clerk, who, apparently employing the transitive property, asked me if I "was a junkie." The sweet doorman went beyond the call of duty and helped me get my things to my room. I tiptoed each bag into the room and lined them up against the wall as British, French, and Irish girls slept soundly in their bunk beds. I couldn't bring myself to scale one in hopes of finding an empty top bunk. I felt I'd made enough noise as it was.

I slipped out to the fire escape and called everyone who came to mind, which was no one. But in an effort to be like Normal People, I called my sister. My sister, like my mom, had been someone I would occasionally call like a reflex because I wanted to be normal, and they would answer, perhaps because they also wanted to be normal. For years, I thought if I just called and ignored all of the things unsaid between us, all of the unspoken pain buried in our conversations where we spoke to each other like former coworkers who hadn't seen each other in years but occasionally caught up, only to talk about the weather, I could pretend I wasn't alone. My mom and my sister were in my phone, which meant I was normal and had a family. But I knew it was a lie.

The best way I can explain this is that, for a long time, some of my relatives were like chewing gum. When you're starving and what you really need on a cellular level is something hearty, something that lasts, something nourishing, something with vitamins, something with minerals, something that will stick to your stomach so the hunger won't return almost immediately but the only thing available is gum, you'll buy gum because it'll mimic the sensation of chewing and eating. But you're not really absorbing or digesting. You will not get full. There are no vitamins. There are no nutrients. And it will never, ever be food. It's better than having nothing at all, but eventually you'll realize you haven't eaten in ages and you're starving. And you'll want a full fucking meal.

As soon as I started to cry, my phone died.

I spread out across the fire escape, hand behind my head, breathed in the cool air, and remembered this was better, any way you sliced it. I used the phone disconnecting to regulate my breathing. I was outside a room with forty sleeping transient girls, just like me, each with their own stories. I lay on the fire escape and stared at the moon, finally allowing myself to cry, and wishing I had someone else to talk to. But I had the moon, and that was fine too.

———

Over the next two months or so, I lived off single-serve boxes of Walgreens dried fruit because it cost about one dollar and worked well enough and no cooking was required.

The hostel was populated mostly by European kids on holiday, and there was a small group of kids I'd see around who seemed to be having the most fun possible. I'd watch them and imagine I was friends with them, which was plenty for me. Just enough socialization without ever having to become actively involved outside my own mind.

One morning, the blond girl in the group came up to me while I was on my laptop in the common area and asked me if she could use my credit card and reimburse me with cash. "They don't let you do a deposit with cash and I don't have a credit card here, bloody idiots," she said. I didn't think twice and gave it to her—who knows why, optimism maybe. She said thanks a million and left.

Later that day in the dining room, she shouted over the tables, "Guys, there's that girl who gave me her credit card number even though I'm a total stranger from another country," in a way that both playfully mocked and applauded me. I shyly motioned *Hi* and the guy in the group, whom I later learned was named Noah, said, "Why would you do that? That's insane. You're really trusting." And immediately I started to imagine that this Irish white girl in her twenties was actually a Middle Eastern prince who had stolen millions from young American punk-rock women because uh, maybe she was? Holy shit. Noah followed up, "Nah, you're lucky. Naimh's cool. I'm Noah. This is Rachel. She's from Greece on holiday. Naimh is from Ireland on holiday. And I'm here from Scotland on holiday. Where are you from?"

Externally, I remained calm and a little reserved, but internally, I was beaming. I was in. I had friends, even for the next five minutes.

"Well, I just moved here, but I rented a room in a crack den full of creepy homeless men and heroin dealers who threatened me when I didn't tell them my name, so I moved all my stuff up here in the middle of the night and now I'm trying to find an apartment that's more populated by people than by roaches and expired vegan snacks."

Externally, they beamed. And from then on, we were inseparable. We went to cafés together, walked ten miles and ordered large vegan pizzas we'd eat individually, went to parties and art gallery openings and museums. I got to see the city as they saw it: as a playground full of endless possibilities, instead of as I saw it, yet another city where I knew no one and nothing, save that I was meant to be here and start my life somehow.

One day, while in a coffee shop in Bushwick, I told Noah about my dream to write for *The Onion* because I loved it and I knew they were based in New York. I knew on some weird level (Stevie Nicks, is that you again???) that I was meant to work there—I just had to figure out how. I had happened upon an ad on Craigslist for *Onion* interns and showed it to him. I had applied, but he told me to follow up in person, why not—and he offered to go with me. I will always be grateful to him for that.

We went over to their Broadway offices in Manhattan and I talked to the doorman. I told him I didn't have an appointment but I was trying to get an internship there and I was sure they got a million applications but I really wanted this and I just needed to try in person. He smiled and told me he had a good feeling about me, and in that moment I felt like Julia Roberts in *Pretty Woman*—without the sex work—and went upstairs.

Not long after, I got the internship, surrounded by fellow interns who lived in $6,000-a-month Park Avenue apartments and had credit cards loaded with $10,000 a month for "expenses," while I'd live off a

$3 miso soup from Dean & DeLuca. One of the interns once turned to me when we were eating lunch there together and said, "That's three dollars? Wow, I didn't even know they had anything that cheap here," and I laughed because she sounded like a rich person in a cartoon. But who cares, because several months after that, I got the writing fellowship and a string of "Congrats, kid. This was the best writing packet we saw, hands down" emails from my now coworkers that came with it. And the knowledge that I was right all along, that I was right to believe I was a comedy writer and I could do this, I was ready, confirmed.

Aaaand then came the news that it paid, like, two hundred dollars a month for full-time work, which was a third of what I'd been told by people that it paid. I guess they cut the pay drastically because . . . fuck it. Having just come off a four-month, nearly full-time internship that paid absolutely nothing, having this full-time position pay next to nothing felt like a punishment in the most delightful form, but a punishment nonetheless. I know now that these industry practices are put in place with the assumption that everyone in the arts comes from a wealthy family who will bankroll them for The Opportunity, thereby shutting out people who have families but don't have money, or people who don't have anyone at all, and however you feel about that concept, it ultimately results in a loss of art from some of the people I want to hear from most.

We don't give the people who don't have the right connections and supreme wealth the map to where the opportunities are, and then when they forge a path there themselves, against immense odds, we charge them a fee for admission we know they can't afford. And then we reward incredibly fortunate, connected, and bankrolled creators without acknowledging there was almost no way they would ever fail. Again, I don't begrudge anyone who comes from a super-supportive family, or a super-wealthy family, or a super-wealthy AND supportive family, but it is so important to remember that having a support system, having a safe, loving family who encourages you and guides you and financially supports you, giving you a safe place to fall—these are luxuries. They should be something we're all entitled to and we all get, but they are not. And even if you have a safe, loving family but no money, you still have guidance and support and a fallback plan of some kind just because they exist. But if you don't have a safe, loving, supportive family guiding you through life AND you don't have money, you're twice as alone.

And if you are one of those people, you will take jobs because you need the money, even if it puts you years off your career path because you don't know any better and if you don't survive, you die. You won't ask for more money when they offer you a starting salary because no one told you to do that. Who would've told you? Your parents? Not a thing. You will have jobs straight up not pay you at all for days, sometimes weeks of work, and you will have no one to call who will say, "That's illegal. Here's what to do," or even "No, I'll call them." You won't have that cool thing where your parents protect you from people taking advantage of you: "She's with us. She has people. Try this shit somewhere else, but not with our girl." The dream.

You will have exorbitant medical bills come in for services they never ultimately performed, and you will spend nearly a year's salary to pay them off immediately because you are scared, because no one is there to tell you that if it's more than your salary, you often don't have to pay. You will spend years patting walls down for a secret doorknob to where you want to be in your career, while people who have one or both of the aforementioned luxuries will see the door clearly and may even have someone point it out to them and hold it open for them.

I hear friends and colleagues say it all the time, how nothing they've done would be possible if it weren't for their family, and a knot forms in my stomach and sometimes it's so sharp I check for physical bleeding. This is not petty envy, not about who is right and who is wrong; it is simply a cigarette-burn-to-the-arm reminder of what I could've had and didn't. And it kind of blows my mind and breaks my heart to think about who I would've been, what I could've done, how much better I could've lived, how much more protected I would have been if I'd had that too.

I guess I just had this idea in my mind that the arts were filled with people like me—little kids with dreams and less-than-ideal families who went off on their own with thirty dollars in their pocket and the determination to succeed. And they are not. It will always confuse me that we don't talk about the difference that makes in our world, the vastness of which I can't even imagine.

I talked to one of the editors there about how I couldn't financially afford it and he told me he thought I should still take it, and if I did, he'd buy me a huge bag of rice and a bulk container of hummus and some beans to live off of. I took the job, but man, I really should've followed up on that food offer too, whether it was serious or not, because in retrospect, that would've helped.

The first time my name was in *The Onion*'s print newspaper, which they had at the time, and it had my first headlines and stories in it, I had no one to show—almost. I *did* have the guy at the Korean deli named Mark who was always the friendliest person in the world. We'd talk every day while I bought vegetables. He was so proud of me and said, "That's so great, Lane!" while I paid with change because I was still hilariously broke, but I felt rich as shit because I was getting paid to write comedy. Sure, it was in nickels, but comedy nickels, which I think are actually less valuable than regular nickels, but still.

I'VE ALWAYS RELIED ON THE KINDNESS OF STRANGERS, BUT, LIKE, IN A SAD WAY

The most tender place in my heart is for strangers.
I know it's unkind but my own blood is much too dangerous.

—NEKO CASE, "HOLD ON, HOLD ON"

I've always had incredible stranger luck and I've never understood it. Stranger luck has appeared in my adult life in such bizarre and fleeting but greatly appreciated ways, often coming and going in a way I perceived as normal. Help, if it came at all, arrived in short bursts, so I just had to savor it as much as I could, because I knew it would end and that would be that. I never got too comfortable or stayed too long, for fear of messing something up and having them take away the help altogether. Better to leave after they've been nice to me for three seconds, because what if this is a trick and staying for a full five seconds results in a punishment? Also, real quick, what is unconditional love?

Due to making so much less than minimum wage at *The Onion*, you guys, just so much, I started using the shit out of Craigslist "free" and Freecycle to get the things I needed. I wrote to one woman about a coat she was giving away because I needed a coat and didn't care where it came from or what it looked like because it was already full-on winter, and that's how I met Rosa. Rosa was an elderly woman who lived nearby whom I quickly hit it off with. She had the brightest and best laugh. I would hang out at her home and watch *American Idol* reruns with her every week while trying to gently encourage her to pursue her long-held dreams of being a painter, which had been cut short due to her ailing parents.

She'd find old furniture on the streets in the city and fix it up. She had this gorgeous 1940s school desk that she'd painted bright red. It was my favorite thing. One day she offered it to me, and after letting her offer it to me six more times because I was worried if I accepted it, she'd hate me—a remnant from my delightful childhood—I accepted and borrowed a hand truck from her neighbor to wheel it over to my apartment. I sent her a photo of me sitting in it, beaming. I wrote on that desk every day for years and kept ideas for jokes and songs in the compartment in the bottom. It was my favorite thing, and I'd frequently send her photos of me enjoying it throughout the year, the way someone who adopted your dog sends you photos of the dog, happy and loved, as it grows older. I ran into her on the street years later and found out she'd gone back to art school. I couldn't have been happier for her.

My other "friends" at the time included Dennis, a landlord who also ran a funeral home and looked out for me in general, but especially once he realized I didn't have anyone else. One day, on Christmas Eve morning, I remember getting a call from him saying, "Come downstairs." I was fucking terrified that I was in trouble or someone was dead, and I asked him several times to tell me why so I could prepare myself, and my fight-or-flight response, to act accordingly. "Just come down," he insisted. I did, cautiously, and he handed me a small box. "Merry Christmas." I looked at him, severely confused, and opened it. It was a silver men's watch with gems surrounding the face. I started crying immediately as he said, "Everyone deserves to have something to open on Christmas." My heart exploded.

My stranger luck first started when I was living in my car as a teenager right after I graduated from high school, like all my fellow teens did for sure (no). I had always been on my own, my own entity, and never belonged to anyone; why would that change now that I was (almost) legally no one's problem?

I didn't have any money, so much so that one time I remember being down to my last five dollars and having to choose between tampons and grape juice, a classic teen problem! But at least I had two jobs and a car to live in and a band that was . . . technically a band.

Nobody can say I did not try to find age-appropriate band members as soon as humanly possible. I did everything I could. I posted online looking for musicians to play with but mostly saw ads looking for "males only" or "MUST BE HOT." While I thought of myself as a cute-enough human, I didn't want anyone to ask me, "How'd you join the band?" and then have to answer, "Well, they said, 'Must be hot,' and I was." Not when I'd spent my whole childhood locked in the bathroom practicing to play in a band. I never looked at it like practice—more like preparation for ~*my destiny*~. I couldn't have known that my immediate destiny would involve a band called Penis Envy, aka a group of aging accountants.

Before I found the members of Penis Envy (WHICH I DID NOT NAME), one of my teachers in school told me he'd seen my post on some punk-rock message boards looking for bandmates and offered to form a band with me. I found this, then and now, to be creepy. That said, he was my favorite teacher in retrospect and believed in my brain when not many other people did, so I will forever love him, even if it was kind of weird that he asked to play music with an underage girl in his class.

Penis Envy was different. For one thing, I was currently a free agent living in my car and living the dream. You know, if the dream is something that started off seeming fun and then immediately became depressing, leading you to a suicide attempt in an airport parking lot. Dreams are different for us all.

I found their ad, clear as I can recall, among the hordes of posts for "Metallica cover band seeking someone looking to rawk" and "Influences include: Green Day and Rage Against the Machine. Men only" listings. Theirs said, "Seeking female lead singer," which back then, and even now, was like seeing a pile of money on the ground and watching everyone walk by it. It shouldn't be there, it makes no sense there, how does it exist, and is it a prank? I replied, listing my musical influences and sending some songs I'd recorded on my computer, and eventually drove in my car/house to their shitty practice space by the grocery store (whose parking lot doubled as my sleeping place, and by sleeping I mean being terrified all night).

I don't remember hearing any of their songs before the audition, and frankly, I couldn't have cared less. I'd spent my whole life wanting to be the front person in a band, and whatever they were serving I would eat, and then some. I just wanted to play music, like it was air and my lungs were collapsed.

When I walked into the audition, I had short hair spiked with Elmer's glue (I told you I was punk rock), and five staples in each ear. (I wore staples in my ear in my teen years and well beyond. I still do sometimes as an ode to my weirdo teen self.) I probably also had on pants that swallowed my body, glitter that dominated my face, and a strict adherence to monochromatic head-to-toe color schemes. And Penis Envy . . . oh, they did not.

I first noticed the lead guitarist, who was a minimum of fifty-seven years old, and then the bassist, who was probably about fifty-two. (The drummer was the "youngest" at forty. I swear I heard one of them joke about how that guy "kept them young" and tried not to look too confused because I was literally in high school two weeks ago, but okay. Who cares.) I'd never sung into a microphone outside of a school auditorium because my dad wouldn't let me use the fifty he had at home because why help your kids find joy? What's in that for you?

They picked a few songs, including Blondie's "Call Me" (not my favorite Blondie song, but I knew it), Cheap Trick's "I Want You to Want Me" (which I had no idea was not originally by Letters to Cleo and absolutely sang that version), Jefferson Airplane's "White Rabbit" (I would've preferred "Somebody to Love," but I also would've preferred to be in a band with people who weren't about to retire). I remember singing quietly at first, since I was still pretty quiet about my music and my singing, never really letting anyone know how hard I was working on building something that would be ready whenever I said so, leave me alone. Now, in this room, I was really doing it—for accountants who probably had kids older than me, but I was doing it. And the more I sang, the louder I sang, because I was finally here, even if it did look very different from what I'd imagined. And I joined the band.

I knew I'd have to play their "originals," which I swear to God were all about taking baths and general home maintenance, but who gives a shit? They let me cover songs by the Cranberries and Letters to Cleo, including their (who knew it was a cover????) version of "I Want You to Want Me." And sure, fine, I'd mumble their stupid bath lyrics until it was time to take over the stage with songs I loved.

In between shows, I'd open up my red Hello Kitty lunch box, filled with my notebooks and a pen and some gum, and I'd write as much as my hands would allow, as I always did whenever I was near paper and a pen. Jokes, poetry, song lyrics, journal entries, keeping a record of everything, all of it, the beginnings of whatever this was. And at the end of the night, I discovered sometimes we got paid (??????) and would take my twenty dollars and buy my favorite cookies at the time, which were the hideously named and insanely delicious Light and Fudgies. These were basically soft, salty sugar cookies with a giant pile of fudge-like frosting on the top and I'd eat them in my car like that was definitely sustainable food for a growing child and try to fall asleep in the front seat, waking up every three minutes to check my windows for murderers.

But it didn't matter. I'd look at the back seat of the car/home with my combat boots lined up in front of the window, making it impossible for me to see cars behind me, and think, "I'm doing it. I'm a musician. This is wonderful." And it was. When you go from a childhood where you're not only painfully alone but often frightened as well, to having the chance to be on your own, even if that means you're homeless in the dead of winter, sleeping in your freezing car in a scary part of town, you'll gladly take it. It's a step up, a comparative paradise. Did I feel safe? No. Had I ever felt safe? No. At least now my life was mine, and I could finally say I was alone and have no one look for the asterisk. And maybe now people would care, maybe then they'd see. But no one ever did.

One night, after hitting a particularly low point in my depression (based on God-knows-what ratio of "my life so far" to "my life at present"), I drove around town looking for answers. I called my childhood Sunday school teacher who had always let me do stand-up every week in front of the class and seemed like she cared maybe, and cried and cried, trying to find a way to make the words not sound so scary, but still important enough for her to grant me help. She just said flatly, "Read the Bible." So I drove to Barnes & Noble and combed through it, visibly sobbing in the religion aisle, as any previously held faith slipped through my fingers like air. I ran through multiple versions as if there would be one version that described my life in literally any way, and advice for how to navigate whatever the fuck this was. All I got was a message that "Jesus has experienced everything you've ever experienced," and I was like, "Um, no, he has not. First off, Jesus had a family. He literally had Mary and Joseph and the Father, and the Holy Ghost. Like, that's a good crew. I'm just saying." And that didn't even begin to scratch the surface of things I'd experienced by the time I finished high school; if Jesus had experienced them, he definitely didn't tell any of the Bible writers, because as far as I could tell, Jesus had a super-trauma-free, family-filled life . . . up until the end.

So I left the store and drove down the street, blasting the Cure's *Greatest Hits* and crying for what must've been the whole night. I think at one point I also stopped by the mall's GNC, where a guy I'd been on one kind-of date with—he looked like an eighteen-year-old Keanu Reeves and was dumb as a brick but also sweet—worked to see if talking to a hot guy with an empty brain would help. It did not.

As I drove, I remember thinking this was the end of my life. This was the day it would end. It had to. Recent events I can't go into—it would shake my whole body and I won't be able to tell you the lighter stuff—had just left me feeling like I would never live to see any of my dreams realized, I would just die, murdered in my car in a parking lot while I shivered myself to sleep. Which is obviously also a very light sentiment. Try bringing it up during tea, I bet it'll land well.

As I drove, I passed a church with the basement lights on, which was weird because it was a Wednesday. I don't know why, but I turned my steering wheel left and pulled into the parking lot and walked into that basement. I have no idea what the women down there thought when they saw a teenage girl with Winona Ryder hair and a "Penny Lane from *Almost Famous*" coat walk in, looking like she'd been crying for a month at least, her face red and hot and her eyes barely able to open so that she can see properly. Or what they thought when I opened my mouth, eyes still mostly closed, and said, "Can I just ask you guys why you don't just kill yourselves? Because honestly what are we waiting for?" To their credit, they didn't yell, "Oh, helllll no!" and leave me there, jumping through the walls like the Kool-Aid Man to escape this random weirdo who was not okay. Instead, they said something about Jesus and Christ's love and I was just not in the mood, but where else did I have to be? So, fine. Go for it, guys.

They asked if they could pray for me and if they could hold my hand, and they prayed for me while I continued to sob until I felt so much I felt nothing at all. After the praying, which I mostly tuned out because that had not worked out for me in the Barnes & Noble either, but it was nice that they tried, they asked me where I lived. I pointed outside and said, "Right out there." And they said, "You live in your car?" and my lip quivered like a child, which I absolutely still was, maybe more than I ever had been before, and my voice shook. "Yeah." One of the women, Abigail, said, "Whew. Okay. So you're not sleeping there tonight. You're going to come and stay with me tonight, and maybe you can go to Miriam's tomorrow, and we'll figure out the rest from there, okay?" I cried again and nodded and followed Abigail to her house down the street. When we got there, I met her husband and their two kids; she had a ten-year-old boy named Ben and a newborn in a crib and I couldn't believe she was letting me stay with her, because I could totally be a murderer. She didn't know. I slept on the couch in the baby's room and readied myself for them to change their minds.

They did not change their minds. They brought me donuts in the morning, which I absolutely assumed were not mine and did not touch them until I was expressly told they were for me, and even then, I picked at them like they were poisoned, or I'd heard them incorrectly.

I stayed with them at night and went to my numerous jobs in the morning and kept out of sight and out of mind, trying not to leave any evidence I'd ever been there, ready at any point to be kicked out, found out, rejected—a foster dog through and through.

I'd play with their son and hold the baby and they'd be kind to me and it would hurt because it was new. I went over to another woman from the church's house and sat on the phone with my punk-rock boyfriend who had a lip ring (so hot at the time) but no emotional intelligence, and talked about how I was literally on the outside of the house looking inside at these people, this family, who moved with one another like they knew choreographed dance steps, and how much it hurt to be an interloper seeing what everyone else had, without even asking.

I stayed maybe three days max because it was too painful and I figured it was better to leave before they could ask me to go and it would break my heart. Before I left, Abigail told me she was going to pray with me, and as soon as she did, she told me, "From now on, any time you go through life, you won't be alone anymore. If you need help or anything, someone will be there to help you. God will send them. You'll never be alone again, okay?" and I smiled at the idea of

that, wanting to believe her. Several days later, on my way to the gas
station, my car made it just short of the station before running out
of gas, and the second I signaled, a car behind me signaled too, and
you guys, it was so fucking weird. I didn't die, I wasn't dismembered,
it was just a dude in his forties who had a feeling I needed help, who
helped me get gas, didn't hit on me, and just went on his way. JESUS
IS MAGIC!!!

In the years since, I've had similar bursts of immediate intimacy
with people I'd just met. A few years ago, I met a lesbian couple,
Colleen and Renée, and their friend, Elizabeth, on the first vacation
I ever let myself truly take, to swim with dolphins. (I adapt so easily
to any kind of communal environment, it's a wonder I've never been
sucked into a cult.) We all made breakfast together and did dishes
together and they laughed at all my weird jokes and they were hippies and grounded and sarcastic and real and no-bullshit and I loved
them. I was the only one there under fifty because apparently once
you hit fifty, and not a day sooner, you're, like, "Time to swim with
dolphins!" and I was absolutely not expecting it to be as touchy-feely
as it was.

While everyone there was openly talking in the sharing circle
about what brought them there, I was the comedian/musician from
New York City in a mustard-yellow grandpa cardigan who holed up
inside herself and would not share, thanks. By the end, I opened wide
as the sun, partly because of the warmth and inclusion and consistency of the very new feeling of seeing someone who liked me and
cared about me every single morning and night. At the end of the
trip, they told me I should come to Atlanta some time and I thought,
"Nah, I'd rather just imagine you're my family in my head rather than
get to know you and potentially feel sad."

But a year later, I took a chance and went. It was incredible. They treated me like family and told me at the end of my stay that during the dolphin trip, they'd all talked and said they felt like they could be a family for me, would love to be that for me. And I cried because I had been adopted like I'd always wanted. But the feeling ebbed and flowed as I grappled with not really being their family, and having that confirmed when I'd later ask when I could come back to see them and they'd say, "Well, the winter won't work because that's the holidays, so we're busy with family stuff." And I remembered who I was. Not theirs. Not anyone's.

The exceptional, overwhelming kindness of strangers who immediately see me and my heart as special and full and open and innately, unequivocally, deserving of love and care right out of the gate, no questions asked, has often left me gut-punched and confused. For years, I'd think that surely my family had to be right about me because they knew me best, they knew the truth: that I was nothing and no one and I was bad and horrible and should've been a baby in a dumpster, good riddance. Strangers were all just fooled by some surface-level magic I was performing—that had to be it—and if I'd spent any further time with them, if they really knew, they'd see it, they'd see the truth that my family was right.

So I stayed away from people and wouldn't get too close to them when they seemed like they wanted to love me and could love me and would love nothing more than to love me—if I'd let them. So I didn't. It would've hurt too much to finally feel loved and then, once they'd realized they'd wasted their time, and I was bad and worthless, to have them leave and come back again, or become unsafe seemingly because the wind blew differently that day, just like my family. No thanks. Better to be alone the way I'd always been.

But now I see it differently. If you're driving on the highway and there's a giant gorgeous garden that's remarkable and special and unlike anything you've ever seen, you'll see it coming from miles away, and even if you see only a flash of it, going sixty miles per hour, you'll know it's incredible. You don't have to spend a ton of time looking at it to know that, and even if you don't inspect it closely, you know what you know and there's no need to question it. It's lovely. The end. But if you're driving past it very quickly and hatefully, to you, it might just be a place where they don't sell any fucking Diet Coke and you really want a Diet Coke, so fuck that place.

My point is, maybe the people who knew me for five minutes and immediately saw how lovable I was saw it because it permeated everything around me and was refracted all around the room, so was clear to anyone who was paying attention. And my family just never was, for various reasons. Maybe they were standing in an art gallery, staring at their phone or looking too closely at paintings, wondering what all these ugly fucking streaks were, what a waste of canvas. But fortunately, those paintings didn't stay in that gallery for long; they left and went outside, where other people could appreciate them and love them and see them and tell them they were perfect and special and they'd very much like to have them in their home.

I LIKED DATING YOU BETTER IN MY HEAD

Perfectly able to hold my own hand
But I still can't kiss my own neck.

—WYE OAK, "CIVILIAN"

Shortly after I started writing for *The Onion,* one of my friends told me he wanted to set me up with someone he thought I'd like who used to write for *Saturday Night Live* but left to go to law school. I loved this concept so much because it meant he was a combination of a lot of things I loved: someone who was theoretically funny and smart but not in comedy at all. Hel. Lo. But then he showed me a photo. At first glance, Everett Roth was a bro-turd with a hipster mustache who looked like he loved away games and rape jokes. I was out. I said no. I said no as politely as I could, but the no was as loud as if I hadn't.

A few months passed and a string of turd-garland dates later, I found myself thinking about Everett Roth. So I googled him until I found some of his YouTube videos. He was lovely. He loved romantic quotes, he had great taste in music, and he spoke with a poetic cadence, which was all very much my shit. And then I found a photo of him looking gentle and sweet and wearing a sweater covered in pink hearts that made my heart stop for at least a full day, no less. And I thought in that instant, "I am going to fall in love with him and also, fuck, this one is going to destroy me." And I did and it did.

I waited patiently for several more months because I was told he didn't come to many of *The Onion*'s Whiskey Fridays because of his schedule. In the meantime, I wrote a song about what I imagined our life together would be like before I even met him. It went like this and was called "Not Very Understandable in French," based on the letter Ingrid Bergman wrote to Roberto Rossellini, thus sparking their courtship.

> I'm feeling good today, there's a lot of things outside I wanna
>   go and see,
> Lot of places that we could go, you and me, if you'd hurry up,
>   come find me,
> I'm feeling happy, I have a lot of things that I would like to try
>   today,
> Things I wanna learn about and demonstrate.
> I wanna be with someone, I wanna be with someone like you.
> Oh, we could rent a boat, go out in the park for hours,
> Or we could walk along the riverside, I hear it's nice in
>   October.
> I wanna be with someone, I wanna be with someone like you.
> Oh, you didn't have to bring me flowers but you did it anyway,
> You know I'm cynical, I'm not that type of girl, that's what the
>   others say.

Oh, but they were wrong. They say I want it all, I want it all.

It's almost autumn I, it's almost autumn I

Wanna try being with someone, wanna try being with
    someone, I wanna try being with someone like you.

So if you have some time and there weren't any plans that you
    had in mind

You wanna go to the park, you wanna stare at the stars.

But there's no one really in town, you haven't found the person
    who would run around.

Oh, I would run straight to you. I would find you anywhere.

It's almost autumn I, it's almost autumn I

Wanna try being with someone, wanna try being with
    someone, I wanna try being with someone like you.

In retrospect, in writing that song, I placed an order for him and that is exactly what I got.

———————

My friend told me that Everett was slated to appear at the upcoming Whiskey Friday, about a week before Thanksgiving. At that point he'd become like the fucking Beatles playing at your local dive bar—a long shot who kept canceling because he probably wasn't coming. I showed up with bells on, and by bells I mean a black dress and a scarf with autumn leaves on it that I'd just bought on my first-ever "vacation" to Montreal (if your definition of a vacation is going to Montreal in the dead of winter and spending all your time working, crying a lot, and listening to "Someone to Watch over Me" while eating coconut bacon in your hotel room).

Once he showed up, I didn't wait for us to be introduced. I

walked right up to him and immediately started talking to him about music and movies, wanting desperately to finally talk to him about all the things I knew he loved, based on his blog, that I also loved, without seeming like "HI, I RESEARCHED YOU AND I KNOW WE'D GET ALONG, BUT, UH, YOU DON'T KNOW THAT AND WOULD IT SOUND CUTE IF I TOLD YOU I'D WATCHED YOUR VIDEOS? OH GOD, YOU'RE CALLING THE COPS AND THAT'S FAIR." I'd been talking to him in my head for so long and was trying my best not to let him know that I'd spent months doing this, anticipating our first meeting.

At one point, one of his friends at the party took a photo of Everett and me talking, saying, "Someone has to document this, holy shit," it was that obvious to everyone around us something magical was happening. And it was. I still have the photo and good luck finding anything cuter.

The only awkward beat in the night was when we exchanged pleasantries about the upcoming holiday and I said I didn't have any family so I didn't do anything for the holidays, and we all quickly moved past it like I'd just said, "My family was murdered in front of me, but what do you do for fun?"

After Whiskey Friday, Everett suggested that we go to a wine bar down the street, so we did, and I remember walking behind him and staring at his black pea coat and immediately wanting to hold his hand, like a magnet was requiring me to do so.

At the end of the night, he told me about a new iPhone app that made you look two hundred pounds heavier than you were, and I will never know why people think this is hilarious, other than a combination of boredom and fat-phobia, but he took a photo of me and showed me how I'd look and then asked for my number so he could text it to me—as a souvenir, I guess? IDK. In retrospect, it just allowed him to get my number in the most bizarre, problematic way possible.

The next morning, and I will never forget this, I had a very, very long email from one Everett Roth that went a lot like this, but very abridged. I wish I had all of the originals, but I tend to lean toward the delete button quick as you can wrong me, even if only by mistake. I have a trigger-happy "erase all evidence of happiness now that you've caused me pain, real or imagined" finger, and I often wish I didn't.

> *Dear Lane,*
> *It was so lovely meeting you last night and I know this is very short notice, but I would love it if you would go on a date with me tomorrow night. I would usually wait a little longer to ask, but my law school schedule being what it is, I currently have more free time than usual and would love it if you'd join me for dinner and a show. I'd love to take you to this restaurant, Chimu, on the West Side. It's modest but very charming. And then after, if you'd like, I'd love for you to join me for a show at UCB. One of my favorite improv teams is performing and it would be really fun. Until then, I've composed this mix for you that will hopefully win your heart in the meantime. I hope you'll say yes.*
> *Sincerely, Everett.*

I was so fucking in. We went to dinner and he was so nervous because they sat us at a communal table with strangers and he hated this so much and was also nervous about how busy the restaurant was because he was nervous we would miss the show (which, as a comedian, I was totally okay with because a random comedy show on a first date is my hell).

I was too nervous because he was too nervous so I didn't eat anything and asked for my meal to go, which was a horrible idea because
by the time we got to UCB, it was just leaking through the bag and I
was just carrying around a loose sauce bag on a first date like a weirdo.
Then we went to get a drink and I probably got some whiskey nonsense that I ordered to sound cool because I was still pulling that shit
back then. The only other things I remember about the date was us
in the bar and his asking me, "So, are you dating anyone else right
now?" and my looking at him like he was insane. I said, "Um, no, I'm
out with you, so." And he said, "Oh, I know, I just wondered if you
were dating anyone else, too."

I'd been in New York City about a year at that point and he
couldn't have known that my dating philosophy, try as I might to
break it in the years since, has always been that if I'm seeing someone,
fuck, even if I like someone and nothing has happened yet, we're on
a journey together and I'm going to see where this goes. It had never
occurred to me at that time that there was any other way to date.

The other thing I remember is him asking me about my exes, and
I mumbled a lot of "Eh, people suck," my abridged version of "I've
been through a lot of shit." And he said, "So you've never dated anyone good?" and I reflexively said no, thinking, "Of course I haven't,
if I had dated anyone good (see: my soul mate only) I'd be married.
What kind of a question is that?" Years later, after having dated far
too many people who had never dated anyone good before me, which
only spelled a world of fucking hurt and work and assignments and
pain for me, I know why he replied, "Oh, dear." He knew what was
to come and I didn't.

I always get very nervous at the end of dates and this one was
no exception. I never know what I'm supposed to do or they're supposed to do, or if they want to kiss me or if I want to kiss them, so

I usually just stare at my shoes until I can literally run away from the moment. Aka I'm fun, date me. This time I just looked at my shoes and said, "Well, that was really fun, I guess normally this is when we'd do something, I don't know, but we're not going to do it because who knows what it is, or if you want to, or if I want to, and we can't know, right? Like, who knows? Anyway, bye." And then I ran to the L train.

I got an email from him the next morning asking me if I wanted to have our second date that Thursday, which was Thanksgiving. He told me he was going to see his parents, who lived in Connecticut, where he grew up, and would happily bring over some food for me afterward. We could hang at my apartment, which was always empty on holidays (which I loved), because my roommates all went home. I told him that sounded lovely but not to worry about the food thing because I had a lot of food allergies, don't worry about it, it's fine (another reflex from my childhood). He said, "Well I can bring some pie then!" and I said, "Well, I just have a lot of food allergies, it's fine," again, terrified he was going to discover I had food allergies and be, like, "Fuuuuck this bitch." I got an email back that said, "Lane, just tell me your food allergies." And so I did. And I held my breath all day when I went babysitting, waiting for him to be, like, "LOL, hell no." He did not.

I readied myself for our second date by listening to, and singing at the top of my lungs and dancing frenetically to, No Doubt's "New," the closest approximation of the way I felt for him, amping up my energy more and more with the refrain "Don't let it go away / This feeling has got to stay." I drank some ninety cups of tea by the time he came over and surely peed twenty times before he rang my doorbell, and I remember so clearly racing up the stairs for our date to begin. He had multiple tote bags, one blue, several that grimy beige tote-bag color that I both love and think should not exist. We got upstairs and he emptied them onto the counter.

"Okay. So! I didn't know what you liked so I brought hazelnut coffee, hot chocolate with soy milk, and apple cider." How was this happening? I had no idea and I swear I dissociated so hard because even now, when I think of it, it makes me nervous. And I know it's just like normal sweetness, but my life had lacked so much of that, and in the past, so many people's attempts at kindness turned out to be motivated by predatory intentions, so instead of just enjoying this lovely date, I kept looking around me for the strings.

———————

He asked me which drink I wanted and I chose the hot chocolate. He took out the second tote bag and said, "There's a bakery downtown that has vegan and gluten-free desserts and I made sure to ask them if they were both and they assured me they are. I got there just as they closed. I was really worried I wouldn't make it in time. I also went to this vegan ice cream shop and got several different flavors that are also gluten-free, I believe. They said they were." He laid out about ten incredible-looking pastries and two pints of ice cream and I want you to know that I've burst into tears while writing just about every single line of this, and it has been years since it happened, because the effects of this second date have still not left my body. This man, this handsome man, left his fourteen-hour law-school day to go to multiple locations the day before Thanksgiving and then left his family on Thanksgiving so he could come be with me and make mine great. And it's the only great Thanksgiving I've ever had.*

* So far (optimism!).

He opened the last tote bag and in it was *City Lights,* which I'd seen before and loved. We brought the baked goods into my big, bright yellow room full of carefully placed knickknacks and sat on my bed, eating them, each one more incredible than the last, and sipping from the various Thermoses he'd brought over. We watched the movie in the way you do on really innocent, adorable perfect first dates—with your whole body tense, desperate to get to the point when you can just hold hands, or put your head on their shoulder or cuddle, but you don't know what to do, so tensing every fucking muscle in your body so you don't accidentally do all three seems like the best move.

The movie was sweet and charming and old-timey and funny, just like he was, just like we were. At some point, we rolled over to face each other and I'm sure I made a series of jokes while looking at my sheets until he kissed me, since that's usually my move. And it was the sweetest, most intense kiss. And, unlike so many kisses before it, it did not immediately devolve into sudden unwanted fingering. Not even close. We kissed for a bit before he pulled away, kissed my forehead, and pulled me close, and said, "Best second date ever." And I remember thinking, "Uh, calm down. It's fine," but only because I knew he was right and I hated him for it. I hated him for being able to absorb how wonderful this was, like, "Oh, yep, this is just what life is like!" without all the dangers of what this could easily devolve into swirling through his head, wits about him, fists up, unwilling to lower them until he was sure he was safe, which could take months or years for all he knew.

I'd spent years trying to use my anxious attachment to my "advantage" in order to become Unreachable Girl. My thinking was, I'd become super unreachable and closed off and terrified, and suitors (I'm calling them that, I just am) would climb that fence because I was worth it. They would get it. They would be patient. And they would work even harder to prove themselves, like people did in countless romantic comedies. That is not what happened.

Not long after this date, I would write a song called "It's Like You're Not Even Trying" with the lyrics "You say, you say there's a fence around me, I'm not letting you in / But I say it's a climbable distance / You just don't wanna put the time in," which was inspired by my constant push and pull with Everett's being annoyed with me for not being able to trust him immediately, and my hating him for choosing to love someone who had been through this much, and then yelling at her when she couldn't shake off a lifetime of trauma and terror she didn't even fully understand, because it would make his life more convenient.

Everett came from a great family. He went to a very fancy elementary school that cost more to attend for one year than I'd made all year, maybe ever at that point. He had loving parents, who are to this day still super in love, and he seemed to genuinely believe nothing bad ever happened in the world. I both loved this about him and hated it so fucking much because he seemed to have no idea life wasn't like this for most people. Everett was eternally sunny and wholly unaware of his privilege, which coupled with his unshakable sunniness made him vaguely punchable.

And his friends were not much better in that respect. Not bad people necessarily, but just very much Rich Young People from Rich Parents with Great Jobs Having Pleasant Conversations over Brie. There's nothing inherently wrong with this, but I've always had a hard time around people who expend a lot of energy projecting perfection. For so much of my childhood, my dad made us fake our way through dinners with his friends, pretending that we were one big happy family. And I wasn't interested in faking it then and I wasn't interested in faking it now. I couldn't get through a dinner without wanting to shout, "I'M SAD. ARE YOU GUYS SAD? CAN WE AT LEAST ACKNOWLEDGE WE'RE ALL KIND OF SAD, AND THEN FINE, SURE, WE CAN TALK ABOUT THE FUCKING BRIE!!!!!!!!!!"

On one such double date, I was seated across from Everett's friend's boyfriend, and Everett was seated across from that guy's girl-friend. The guy and I talked—he was in finance and his girlfriend was in law school, which is how Everett knew her—and he said, "So I hear you're a comedian?" "Yeah, I write for *The Onion*!" I said, beam-ing every time I said it, because I freaking *did*! He sat across from me, looking like what you're picturing: a white guy with blond hair and one of those front-zipper sweaters and khakis who wants you to know he also owns one Rolling Stones album and really digs it.

"Oh, cool. I'm in finance, but I also play a little guitar," he said, in the way that square professional dudes always say to artistic girls. I smiled, still in the phase of being excessively kind to My Boyfriend's Friends, who weren't that great, despite the fact that I hate this and why do we have to do this again? Why can't we just stay home and watch documentaries I don't want to watch but you do want to watch while I sit through them, bored out of my mind, and ohhhh, I see now that this relationship was bad.

Anyway, I told him, "Oh, cool! I'm also a musician!" a very, very generous comparison to give to a guy who I guarantee knows three bars of "Smoke on the Water" max. "Oh, no way," he said, and I could see the boner forming underneath the table, but I told myself I didn't because he had a girlfriend and she was literally right there. I told him I made music and played all sorts of instruments and I called myself It Was Romance and some of it was "kind of online," since I was still very much afraid to let anyone know I did this—like a body builder afraid to admit he also fucking crushes at ballet. What will the community think, etc.? But also desperate for people to hear my music because I loved it so much and really thought it was great.

Eventually he said something to the effect of "Yeah, me and Shana have been together for five years now, since college. We live together. She wants to get married, but I'm, like, eh, I just don't care. But she thinks we're going to. Ha. We're definitely not, though. But, like, it's her first real relationship, so it's a big deal to her or whatever. I've been with lots of girls though, so I'm, like, eh, it is what it is," as he winked at me, like, *Just so you know, she means nothing to me. Sup?*

And I tried not to stare at him bug-eyed like he'd just told me he planned to later put her body in a trunk and bury her outside this bar.

When Everett and I left them and went to the subway, he held my hand and said, "Gah! They're so great, right?! Such a cool couple. They're gonna get married, I just know it. It's so great!" I hesitated to break his confidence in this, since he seemed so happy and so joyful and unblemished by literally any hardships and I wanted to protect him, but I also blurted out, "Welllllll, I'm not sure they are," while we walked to the R train. "What? Awh. No, no, they are! They're so happy. It'll be great." I glared at him like he was a bloated corporation bragging about how it was too big to fail before I added, "He kind of . . . he kind of hit on me. And then told me she cared more about the relationship than he did and he didn't see it going anywhere. And then he literally said he didn't want to marry her. At all." But it wouldn't deter him and he didn't hear me and nothing I said mattered, "Oh, no no no, dear. I'm sure it was a misunderstanding. They're getting married!" And we walked wordlessly to the train and kissed and said goodbye.

Every time I saw Everett, and I mean literally every time I saw him, he brought me flowers. Not bodega flowers. Like, "You ordered these and picked out every single one so it was the most stunning bouquet you could've possibly given me." He started doing this on our third date and did it every date after and never faltered, not once. One time he even came all the way down from a meeting in Harlem to my Brooklyn apartment after a fourteen-hour workday when he had a cold, just to give me flowers because he missed me. He sent me cute packages in the mail constantly, a marker of our "weirdly long-distance relationship because you live in the same city, but you work all the time because you're in the middle of law school, and according to the internet, that's a very hard time to start a new relationship."

I was comparatively poor, but I made up for it with romantic gestures and drawings and songs and maps drawn of where he was and where I was connected by hearts and things like that. And every single time he gave me flowers I made it my full-time job to keep them alive until the next time I saw him, which sometimes was a week or two weeks. On the fourth date, he filled his kitchen, and I mean seriously filled every cabinet, with vegan and gluten-free food. Pancake mix, brownie mix, rice bowls, soup, replacement egg mix, almond milk, just literally everything. And I remember when he showed me all this, I wanted to run. My response, based on some prior, super-fucked-up life experiences, was seriously, "Are you going to force me to date you until all of this is gone????" I can laugh at that now, but at the time, I genuinely perceived it as a threat to my safety, like I had to keep dating him now and he was trying to make me by keeping me tied to him via my food allergies!!!

Suffice it to say, I both desperately wanted him to take care of me like this forever and ever, and also wanted to spit in his face for it because I was so scared that if I accepted this care, my freedom would somehow vanish and I'd be trapped here, unable to say no, unable to leave. I also had seriously deep-rooted fears about men, inherited from my mom.

When I was a kid, my mom described her relationship with my dad as "He was so sweet at first. Always so sweet at first. But then . . ." I have spent my entire life terrified of the "but then." And I spent the entirety of my relationship with Everett worrying that one day, if I got too comfortable, if I accepted the constant compliments about my being the most beautiful girl in the world, the ever-present stunning bouquets, the apartment full of food just for me, and the requests for me to come to lunch with his grandma so she could meet me, a trapdoor would open and inside would be him, ready to beat the shit out of me for falling for it. And so I stayed Fiona Apple "Shadowboxer"-braced, ready for him to fucking try something. And then, when my terror from waiting became too much to bear, I started breaking up with him constantly.

One time I was going to do it over the phone, but I'd left my ice skates at his house like some kind of fucking idiot who feels comfortable with her boyfriend and leaves things at his house and doesn't at all times keep her things in her home in case she needs to run. And while running an errand (to pick up free partially used soy milk someone in his neighborhood was giving away on Craigslist), I decided to surprise him—not to see him, but to get my skates because I Had to Get Out.

It's hard for me to know exactly what caused this constant need in me to run. Sure, it could've been that any time I'd bring up gender double standards, he would be silent, as though I'd said something stupid, and change the subject. Or how I wrote and published a really cool comic book called *Smarty Pants* and gave him a copy that he never read. Or how I sent him my It Was Romance songs as I wrote them, all of them about him and how much I loved him but I never told him that, and he barely listened to them, but could speak for hours about how his accountant buddy did some electronic music "on the side" and it was "so dope." Or how one time he said to me, about some *New Yorker* writer, "God, can you imagine being that great of a writer?" Which stabbed me in the gut and I bled out on the bed while he went to make us heart-shaped pancakes. Or how he handled my telling him that twelve hours after one of my extended family members finally acknowledged the childhood horrors everyone else had constantly swept under the rug, thus finally validating my memories and experiences, she did a 180 and went back to telling me they never happened. His response was "Oh, dear, I'm sure she loves you. Okay, so what sushi should we order?" And I pulled my hand away like I needed it to read the menu, but that was not why. Or how a guy I'd been playing music with suddenly became violent and I told him about it, in tears, terrified and trying to find the words, and his only reply was "That's too bad. I know how much you loved playing with him!" As though he'd quit or moved. That was all. The end.

I can see now that his aggressive lack of support for my career was almost assuredly based on the fact that he wished he was a musician but had no musical talent, and had briefly pursued being a comedy writer but had given it up to be a lawyer. When I first found out the latter, before we met, I thought he was perfect for me. To me, that very mature decision meant he was funny and a great writer but wanted to have a proper normal job, and thus was very stable and deep and compassionate and had the capacity for an enduring and committed relationship, which most male comedians and musicians do not have, in my experience. I don't really know what his motivations for changing careers were, but I truly believe, on some level, he hated dating someone who was going after the dreams he'd given up. And though I tried not to, I hated dating someone who'd had the family, security, and ease I'd always wanted, and acted as though this was something everyone had—who cares, no big deal. I wasn't resentful of his ignorance of how bad the world could be, I was jealous that I'd never in my life had the luxury of that kind of ignorance—the innocence we all deserve to have as children, and ideally as adults. We're all supposed to think, as long as we can, that the world is safe and great and wants us to be happy and that we will always be held and everything will be fine. And I never felt that, not even as a child. And he had and still did. And in that way, we both resented the other for having lives we deeply envied.

Still, there was the other side of him, and it was everything I'd ever wanted. I once saw on his computer that he'd meticulously marked his calendar with future dates like "anniversary of our first date" and "three-month anniversary." He also had a whole bookmark folder on Amazon of things he wanted to buy me, with his search history devoted to things he thought might make me happy. He'd bring a bottle of wine when we'd go to parties and say, "Sweetheart, we're taking them this wine. It's really nice, I just wanted you to know." He would put whole cinnamon sticks in glasses of hot cider. Everett knew how to live comfortably, richly, and well, and he was an adult. And unfortunately I was still a scared little kid who was programmed to merely survive and had no chill.

One time, we got into a fight because we were going to get tea and it was one subway stop away, but, like, five degrees outside. All I could think about was how I couldn't afford to take the subway for one stop just to get tea, but I didn't want to admit that to him. He finally picked up as to why we were suffering through the bitter cold when we could just take a cab or something, and offered to just get us a cab, but I was not having any of it. I couldn't just let him make my life easier; I didn't know how to. I knew how to survive, and if I could withstand something, if it wouldn't kill me, that was fine. And it's heartbreaking to think about.

Everett's love languages (and I know that term is cringeworthy, but still) were gift-giving and service, a potent combination I was immediately drawn to, but I didn't feel like he saw me or really loved me. I didn't learn about love languages until years later, but if I'd known about them then, I would've known why we didn't work. Currently, my love languages are gift-giving, service, and compliments. But at the time, service was definitely not on that list, since I held on so tightly to my I CAN DO IT BY MYSELF I HAVE ALWAYS BEEN BY MYSELF OKAY I HAVE THIS LEAVE ME ALONE beliefs with a freaking death grip.

And because Everett's love languages didn't include compliments, and when they did, they were pretty much just about my appearance and nothing else, I felt with him the way I'd felt with various men I knew back home. Many of these men who would also go on to become lawyers and doctors begged me to stop pursuing "this thing." They each told me I should just move back home and live with them and we could get married and have a good life and I could "write in my spare time," like it was some bullshit thing I could do when I wasn't waiting for them to come home for dinner, because *Mad Men* is very much alive and well.

I was spending so much time surrounded by guys at comedy shows or guys in my band, who saw what I could do, how quickly my brain worked, how quickly I could write incredible songs or entire bits, or dive into characters, or write increasingly spot-on *Onion* stories and were attracted to me because of that. I was really coming into my own . . . but to Everett, I was seemingly the pretty artist girl who was so ambitious at whatever and stuff.

And it began to change me. I started going to the salon more. (Note: These were stylists I found on Craigslist who were in need of hair models, because I could not afford that shit). I started making sure I always looked perfect, no flaws, no scratches. Looking back, it was like my soul had left my body and I had, without even noticing, morphed into what I, on some level, felt he wanted: a Real Housewife, if Karen O had been a Real Housewife. Me, but watered down so I wasn't so much trouble.

And every time I'd leave his apartment, I'd cry the whole way home, all while carrying stunning bouquets half the size of my body, thus making me look like I was always on my way to or from a funeral. I see now that I was overwhelmed by the weight of not being able to tell him what I needed, physically, emotionally, sexually, or what I didn't want, physically, emotionally, and sexually, because I had no idea what was going on inside my head. I didn't know if this was as good as relationships got or if I just wanted too much. And so I constantly left, but felt so devoted and attached to him that I would always come back and he'd take me back every time. I'm sure it exhausted him, but what he didn't know was, it was exhausting me too.

If I met him now, I'd be able to better communicate the issues I had, be able to explain why I got terrified when he'd do certain things, be able to ask him to do things differently, to be able to examine his belief systems and the ways he did or didn't support me. And maybe it would've gotten better. But it was too much to unpack and it hadn't gotten bad enough on paper for me to get gone and stay there.

As Valentine's Day neared, so did his birthday, and FYI, I had been preparing for that for months. I had a weirdly competitive streak for a long time about being the most romantic, movie-moment-creating person ever, I think partly as a challenge and partly as a chance to show my partners, "Yo, this is the kind of love I want, FYI, but also look how much I love you!!!"

So my idea for his birthday celebration was—you know—that thing where maybe it's your birthday or just a hard day or something and you're out somewhere and they play one of your favorite songs and you feel like the whole world exists for you and is rooting for you and you're held and loved and the day is truly yours? I wanted to make a playlist of songs he loved deeply and then tell the bar where we were going to go to put the CD on and he wouldn't know I made it, so he would just be endlessly happy and feel like life loved him and believed in him and this night was truly for him and he was special and great.

I did this through a series of strikingly sneaky questions in person, but also by going through his old music blog from college, which had, Jesus, I think four hundred fucking pages of archives, and was done with two of his friends, so I had no way to sort by author; thus I had to read through every page to find the songs he'd written about in order to compile my mix. I also pulled some strings via some adults I knew to get tickets to see one of his favorite bands and made sure to get tickets to a show that took place on a night where he didn't have finals or a super-hectic week so he could truly enjoy it. And this was just for his party. On the day of his actual birthday he was studying at home and couldn't meet up so I came to him with his favorite drink and his favorite cake to surprise him while he worked. And we also made out a lot. So, win win win.

Prior to his birthday party, I'd called a bar I thought would be the perfect location for him and all his friends because he told me he didn't have time to plan anything, so I handled it all, happily. I went into the bar and told them we were going to be having a ton of people there for my friend's birthday and asked them to play the mix—and they said yes! (I didn't want to say "my boyfriend" because I'm pretty sure, after several months, I still felt scared to let him call himself that, though he'd wanted to since day one and had been waiting, confused but patient, for permission ever since. Also, I knew being like,

"OMG I wanna do something kewt for my boyfriend!!!!" might not foster compassion in a skeezy bar run by misanthropes.)

The day of his actual birthday party, he'd decided everyone would go to his friend's house (one of the Brie and Small Talk couples) before the party to hang out and drink. I asked him what time we'd move to the bar and he said, "Eh, who knows. I just figure we'll hang there and go over eventually." I couldn't ask for further specifics without him knowing, so I spent the pre-party pacing, surrounded by a ton of people I didn't know, watching the clock, knowing my friend Sachi was waiting at the bar for me at nine and the CD-playing guy was probably, like, "Where's this weird girl who is supposed to tell me to play this so I can do it and then jerk off to the idea of being in the band Ratt?"

I didn't have their number to call them because I didn't have an iPhone when literally everyone else did because, again, I was an unpaid/underpaid artist at the time, so I called my friend Nik in LA and had him google the number so I could call them. And this was in the 2010s, not the 1980s like it sounds. Poverty is very retro.

I told the bar in a hushed tone, like I was planning a hit-and-run inside the Brie Couple's bedroom, where I could almost guarantee they'd had sex once this whole year max and yawned throughout it, that I was running a little late and asked if they could just hold off and hopefully we'd be there soon, and then I ran back in to see Everett like I was a waitress juggling too many tables.

"Hey! So my friend Sachi is at the bar and I told her I'd meet her there. Do you know if we're gonna head over soon?" I said, super casual, suuuuuper casual. "Awh, you know what sweetheart? I might just stay here. Everyone's having so much fun, and I just feel really great about it and why even leave?" UH, BECAUSE I'M ABOUT TO BE SUPER FUCKING ROMANTIC?!! MAYBE BECAUSE

OF THAT??!?! WHAT THE SHIT, DUDE??!?!?! But I did not say that. Instead I said, "Word. But Sachi's there and I told her to meet me there and I feel bad."

"Oh. Okay, yeah, we can head over in a few minutes, then. No problem." THANK FUCKING GOD.

So we start walking the few blocks to the bar and everyone is taking their sweet time and it is fine because I have a plan and it is about to happen and he's gonna be so fucking happy and he will know I love him and he will realize I am awesome and he will grab my face and kiss me passionately and say, "Jesus, you're the best girlfriend in the whole world. Holy shit. I can't even . . ." and then maybe hopefully cry.

We get to the bar and, like someone confirming a hit on someone, I coolly nod to the bartender, who goes to put on the CD. We hung out by the bar with his friends and I'm waiting and it's not coming on soon enough, come onnnnn. And then it does!!! The first song comes on and he doesn't notice and I nudge him and say, "Oh my God, dude, do you hear this?" and he says, "Yeah!" and I smile and I love him so much and I am so glad I get to do this for him because I know I'm a tough nut to crack and he's so patient and handsome and good to me, even though he does have some flaws but like who doesn't and nothing is perfect and yesss the next song is playing now and I made such a great mix, I really did.

Several songs in, while he was singing me lyrics to the Tribe Called Quest song "Jazz (We've Got)" and holding both my hands as it played over the speakers, his preppy guy friend (seriously, is there a clown car full of them at this party somewhere?) came up behind us to tell him, "It sounds like you made this playlist, bro," and I could not contain myself anymore. I turned to Everett and said, "Hey! Okay, so this playlist. Uh, I made it." He looked at me confused for a second, and I kept waiting for him to be like, "Wait, WHAT???" and then

I'd tell him and he'd movie-kiss me and know I loved him and we'd be together foreeeeever. What actually happened was he waited two seconds, put it together, and said, "Oh, cool," and hugged me briefly and then went back to talking to his friends about the "sick mix." Sachi was watching nearby and looked totally stunned, like she'd just watched him punch me in the face. "Wait, what the fuck was that?" and I just said, "I don't know," trying to hide the lethal mixture of embarrassment, heartbreak, disappointment, and the rejection of a love I'd finally found the courage to express.

I sat in the corner the rest of the night, which he didn't notice at all. I can still see myself in that corner, sipping water from a tiny plastic cup, watching him move through his sea of bland popped-collar bros from college like I didn't exist. His friend Mike started asking me how I knew Everett because I looked that foreign and out of place that even a stranger was, like, "Yeah, this bitch is barely in his life," which was a very cool feeling after putting the whole party together and working on the mix for months, coupled with him getting angry at me for not letting him in sooner and then the second I did, pushing me aside like a shitty wilted garnish that's getting in the way of the burger he ordered.

I tried to put it aside and assume he was just not thinking, it was fine, and anyway I still hadn't told him about the tickets I got to see the band he loved, so before he left, I tried him again, like a fangirl trying to get the attention of a band she liked. "Oh, hey! Uh, so before you go, I got you tickets to see Röyksopp. I was going to get you tickets to see Toro y Moi, but I looked at your calendar and that would've overlapped with finals, so I didn't want you to be stressed about that, but the Röyksopp show is right after finals, so you can celebrate being done and not even have to worry about it!" His reply was "Hm. I think I can make that."

And then he left me there while he went back into the city with his friends. He didn't walk me home, which was literally two blocks away. I don't even think he kissed me goodbye. I went home and criiiiied and knew I had to end it, and then beat myself up because maybe I was wrong and too sensitive.

When you don't have a support system, being patient while waiting for a soul mate is fucking impossible. So if you have someone in the ring at all, even one stick of shitty gum that gives you a stomachache, it still feels so much better than nothing. And in so many ways, he was such a great stick of gum. He was always cooking for me, always paying for dinner, always making me feel like someone was finally, finally, taking care of me. Having that kind of consistency and someone taking care of me on any level, even if he was thoughtless at times, was a huge step up, and it felt ungrateful to want more than this, so much more.

The next morning, Everett called me like nothing was wrong because to him, nothing was. I tearfully told him that I was really sad last night because I'd worked for months on this party and he acted like he barely cared. He told me that wasn't true, that he was "pretty sure" after I told him about the mix that he'd kissed me. I said he had not. He said, "Really? I think I did!" Nope. You didn't. "Huh. Well it made me feel amazing. I felt like I'd won a thousand lotteries. You're the best girlfriend anyone could possibly have." I said, "Yeah, see, this would've been cool to hear last night. And why didn't you come home with me or even kiss me goodbye?" He told me he was just overwhelmed with how many people were there for his birthday and he wanted to make them all happy because they'd come so far to see him and he wished he could've gone home with me—again, something that would've been nice if he'd said it before leaving with his entourage without even a miming of "I gotta go, but I don't want to, you're the best, I love you so much," with hand signals. Still, in his mind, he'd said his "Oops," and then asked me where I wanted to go to dinner that night, like, "Case closed. I told you whoops, whoops was admitted, so, sushi?"

He then mentioned that he'd left something at his friend's house from the night before and asked if I could swing by and pick it up and bring it to him when we went to dinner. I said sure, feeling officially like an unpaid TaskRabbit, instead of a girlfriend doing something for her boyfriend because she loved him and she knew he loved her.

I cried the whole walk over and wiped my tears away just before ringing the doorbell, but in that way where you're kind of praying they can tell you were crying and ask you about it. She did not. She handed me the extra wine or whatever the fuck it was—honestly, who cares?—and said, "So, are you and Everett doing anything for Valentine's Day?" which was a few days away. I said, lump in my throat—again "Please please notice I am not okay, I am forbidden from asking for help due to shitty patterns from my childhood, so please let me know it is okay to ask"—"Oh I'm sure we're not." She said, light as a feather, "Oh, I'm sure you will!!!!" and I looked past her, to the wall, and said, "We won't. Trust me. Okay, thanks." And left.

I called him to tell him I'd picked it up, and he said, "Great! Thank you!" and I gave him a five-star rating on his TaskRabbit account.

WHAT IF THIS IS AS GOOD AS IT WILL EVER GET: SETTLING AND YOU!

What more can I give you to make this thing grow?
Don't turn your back now, I'm talking to you.

—PATTI SMITH, "PISSING IN A RIVER"

"I'm so excited for you to meet these guys," Everett said while changing his sweater and my staring at him and thinking how truly fucking beautiful he was, but never saying it because you can't let them know they are everything to you. That is how they leave.

At his birthday party a few weeks back, one of These Guys made a joke about his weight and how he was scrawny and had no muscle and turned to me and said, "You need to feed this guy better," simultaneously body-shaming him and turning me into a fifties housewife who was a lazy bitch. Everett laughed and I got protective-bulldog angry and said, "He's fucking perfect. There's nothing wrong with him," and his friend said, "Okay, okay, damn. Calm down," and I seethed. Because I really did think he was perfect and I hated his frat-guy friends who made him feel like shit, like it was a punch line, and how polite and repressed he was about all of it.

We walked to Night of Joy from my house, and when we got there, the guys were at a table by the front. I wished I were at home watching TV.

At one point, the subject of *The Onion* came up. Everett hadn't written for *SNL* in years and I was writing for *The Onion* all the time. One of the guys turned to Everett and said, "So, do you know anyone over at *The Onion*? Are they going to move to another city or what?" and then turned to me and said, "You know, a lot of girls would be really jealous of you and would love to be in your position. Everett's in law school AND he writes for *Saturday Night Live*." "Wrote for. Past tense," I thought, bitter about the implication that I wasn't good enough and should thank my lucky stars I had such a Good Guy, as though I was nothing and no one, just a dumb girl who probably didn't even appreciate their friend who was a god blah blah blah whatever. Everett replied nervously with, "Well, I actually haven't been writing for *SNL* much lately, but Lane writes for *The Onion*. She would know if they're moving." I immediately realized he'd been telling his friends he still wrote for *SNL*, that he could do it all, that he hadn't given up his dream of being a writer at all—no, no, of course not. He was just adding "lawyer" to his fully manageable plate.

They heard his redirect, looked at me, and decided, "Eh, fuck that," and turned to him again to ask him if *The Onion* was moving, a guy who clearly knew more than I did about MY JOB THAT I HAD AND HE DIDN'T. When we parted ways and he went home with the guys, I said nothing.

Later that night, I called him. I told him how shitty it felt and how, um, kind of sexist his friends were for assuming he knew more than I did, presumably because he was a man, even after he'd ad-

mitted he had no clue what was going on there. I tried to explain
to him how much this was definitely A Thing—and he got so angry
and started yelling. I can see now he was yelling at me because I had
caught him in a lie.

Once again, I'd gotten to the root of all the reasons we never quite
worked: because I was doing everything he wished he could do and
he hated me for it. And on some level, I knew that and continuously
made myself smaller and quieter and prettier, yes dear, to please him.
Just as my mother had done with my father. And when I didn't do that,
when I spoke up, spoke out, got louder, achieved more, he would then
make me smaller and quieter again by not acknowledging any of it and
reminding me that I was nothing and he loved me so much.

He ranted and yelled about how he "believed women shouldn't pay
for their own rape kits" and how he would "vote against it every time,"
using this bizarre non sequitur as evidence he wasn't sexist, which I
never said he was, and only said his friends seemed to be in that in-
stance. I begged him to stop yelling at me and told him if he was going
to keep doing it, I would have to get off the phone, trying to handle
him with love and respect because I don't believe in blindly hanging up
on people you love, even when you should. He did not do the same.
He yelled as much as he wanted to and hung up on me as soon as he
got the last word. And I was done. This was it. I felt like I had met the
monster my mom warned me was inside even the best of men.

The next day he texted me like nothing had happened. I told him
I was not ready to talk. He didn't listen and called me. I said I did not
want to talk yet. He yelled at me again. I said this is why I didn't want
to talk yet and hung up and cried.

I've always wished that people who had hurt me would magically
text me: "Hey, I noticed you were upset, and instead of assuming
it was nothing, I took the initiative to reexamine my behavior and

realize I was being a jerk. Because I did this, I'm sparing you the emotional labor of explaining to me how I hurt you. Here are action steps for how I'll make it right." But so far it's been just me and a five-hour conversation I have to initiate, on top of being hurt, and it makes you want to never date again.

He texted me and called me and begged to come over, but I was done. I told myself he never really cared about me and now at least I knew it. I was truly convinced, via my PTSD-brain, which was wired and ready to perceive violence and danger in any form, that his yelling at me was evidence he'd kill me if he could and I had to get to safety. He told me, "Please let me come over so you can look at me and I can look at you and you can see that I care about you." Looking back, I wish I had. Kind of. But I didn't.

I wrote him a furious letter calling him out for all of it, just scathing and angry, making everything black-and-white in my mind, a skill I'd learned in order to keep myself safe. "Safe, Unsafe, there is no third option, Lane, run!"

He wrote me back telling me these last five months had been the best of his life and that I meant the world to him and that he knew he was a good boyfriend to me. I angrily wrote back, chastising him for patting himself on the back for how great he was to me.

I thought he would fight for me. I thought he would see through the pain I was in, and he would know that I'd seen us getting married and never thought we'd truly end, that he'd come to my door with flowers and an apology that let me know he truly heard me and things would be different. But he didn't.

That night I grabbed my ukulele and hit record on my phone, and wrote a song—"But Not Forgotten"—that would later be on my band's first album. The original improvised version was about eleven minutes long and full of crying. It was everything I'd wanted to say to him but couldn't. The final version on the album is barely, if at all, altered, save for the deletion of, like, six minutes of crying. I knew exactly what I wanted to say and said it. And in the years to come, and sometimes even now, I would cry every single time I played it at a show.

We met one last time at a Starbucks in the city and I told him I wanted to get back together. He sighed and told me that was what he wanted to hear more than anything in the world, but he didn't think it was a good idea. He told me he didn't think he was good enough for me. He told me he wasn't a violent man and that he never yelled and couldn't believe or forgive himself for yelling at me. He admitted that law school had made him cruel and ill tempered and inattentive to things he should've noticed, should've given me, should've been present for. And maybe after law school was done . . .

And with those words, I held on forever.

We kept talking every day and I transformed fully into a 1940s army wife, desperately, patiently waiting for his tour of duty to be over so we could be together. He would still send me songs and still called me by the pet names he'd given me. He'd tell me about law school and say things like, "Laney! Class was so great today. One of the teachers is an environmental lawyer and told me that once law school was over he had a pretty manageable nine-to-five schedule and could actually see his family!!!" I heard this and thought, "He wants me to know that if I just wait a few years we can have a family. So I will." And so I did. I waited and wrote song after song about him, cried and cried, isolated myself, and posted YouTube videos of cover songs meant for him. I lived for him for years, and just barely. And mostly through my music.

I wrote an upbeat but frantic It Was Romance song called "Come Home" about how brutal being apart from him in this uncertain, paralyzing way was. The song includes lines in which I reference barely being able to function without someone, all with a catchy pop-rock beat you can really groove to!!! I wrote a song called "Cold War," in which the first line is "There's blood in my teeth again, there's blood on the floor again." Truly, so many songs about Everett were heavy with blood references. In happier moments, I wrote "Philadelphia," a nod to sixties pop, about calling Everett and his picking up on the first ring—"I wanted to tell you everything, but it was too sad." The whole song is my singing about how if he got picked up at a practice in Philadelphia, I would've followed him there and left everything behind. I'd already mentally left everything in my life; why not just pack up and go? Healthy decisions left and right!

Both "Chances" and "But Not Forgotten" end with references to what I'd wanted most from Everett, for him to come running back to me, flowers in hand, just like in the movies. Those have always been the scenes that killed me most, the ones where someone has hurt someone or let someone down, but then, just in the nick of time, there's a knock at the door and an acknowledgment of everything that the person has done wrong, and everything you needed and will now get: a kiss and a chance—nay, a promise—of a future.

I started losing a lot of weight and was eating only one salad a day, with sundried tomatoes, olives, red peppers, salt and pepper, and avocado. That's all. This was the only salad I ate for months, maybe even the whole year. It took a while for me to realize it, but the last night we'd had together, truly had together before the stupid drinks/hang with his friends, we'd watched movies and made a salad together with sundried tomatoes, olives, red peppers, salt and pepper, and avocado. And my brain so desperately wanted to get back to the last night I'd ever have with him that it tried to pause time by wanting nothing but that salad for a year. Subconsciously, I thought that maybe if I ate it enough, it would rewind time, and he would be holding me again and we would be fine.

I lived in this middle place with him, with us talking all the time and then not at all, and when he would disappear, I'd dive deep into websites for people dating or married to lawyers. I'd post all over message boards about our situation, praying that I was just one of these lawyer's wives who just had to be patient and put her life on hold and wait until he was ready. The message-board users mostly disagreed, though. "I don't know. I'm in third year too, and I don't see my girlfriend much, but I can't imagine life without her. We just make it work." And again I felt broken, not worth it, a benchwarmer who might never be sent back out to play again but who had nowhere else to go.

In those years, I truly don't remember anything but crying and writing songs about him and waiting for him to choose me. This makes me very, very angry and sad.

We'd see each other here and there for coffee and he'd act like we were old friends and I lived in Holland now or some shit, acknowledging none of the difficult parts of this, or what this was exactly. We'd meet up at the diner by my house, or go see the new Werner Herzog movie together and get an awkward cup of tea after. We'd act like we were still dating, but when I'd try to push past whatever curtains seemed to be in front of who we really were, and what was really happening, he would shut down and pull away. I'd cry and ask how this was so easy for him, how he could act so casual. And he told me robotically, "It *is* hard for me. But I just have to put it on a very high shelf because I have to get through the day and get through work." That high shelf was not reachable for me, but he was taller than me, so maybe that was why.

We'd always expressed ourselves in such radically different ways and I just trusted that he was mine and always would be, and that all of the spaces we occupied in between were his needing time, his getting through law school, and my putting my whole life and, inadvertently, my career on hold to wait for him like a war bride.

I got hired to be a comedy editor around this time, freelance, like so many websites loved to do it. ("Hey, can you manage eighteen websites and work twenty hours a day for a shitty freelance rate, no benefits, and a huge-ass taxation at the end, even though this is one thousand percent a full-time executive position? Thanks!!!") But it was better than the (maybe) $500 a month I was making working for multiple sites. I took it. I worked in the West Village, just blocks away from one of the practices he was working at, and a quick train ride from another. I walked by the one near work every day on my break, hoping I'd see him—essentially stalking someone I was technically absolutely still dating. We'd never ended it, simply hit the pause button, then the start button, then pause. So I kept showing up, via email, via text, via phone calls, via walking by his workplace, hoping it was time.

One day I even went to the grocery store and bought him a bunch of food and brought it to his office and left it for him at the reception desk with a note attached. He got it and said thank you so much and told me about his day and I just really loved him. We kept on doing this "kind of dating" for two years, despite my noticing, "You say you have no time, and if you did, you'd spend it with me, but the internet exists and I see you doing things without me, so why won't you just keep me or let me go?" Two years. It was beyond cruel, and I can see that only now. Throughout that time we didn't kiss, we didn't hold hands, we just existed in between, with him acting like everything was as it always was, and me playing along and crying the whole way home.

I felt like it was a puzzle I had to constantly solve. I couldn't leave, because he was still talking to me like a girlfriend, was writing to me semi-regularly, and we saw each other semi-regularly. Going on the second year of this fucking bullshit, I emailed him and told him, "I can't keep doing this. Either just be with me, or let me go. Please." And he replied with a bunch of circular nonsense about how being with me was the most incredible time period in his life and he was sure life would never get better than what we had, and then said words that rang in my ear like a high-pitched noise that hurts your ears forever. "You continue to be the most ever-looming presence in my life, and I can only hope you'll stay that way." WHAT THE FUCKING FUCK DOES THAT MEAN, YOU FUCKING ASSHOLE??? So I wrote back, and I was angry, livid. And I yelled at him. And I regretted it at the time, thought it was too mean. Now I kind of don't. You can't tell someone they're all you think about and want, while they wait in a convent for you to actually be with them in any real way, and try to wrap up that box of bullshit in some mildly well put nonsense.

Looking back, I see that all of this was so textbook tied to my family dynamics that it makes perfect sense I couldn't let it go, for different reasons each time. I couldn't let it go the first time because it was a secure attachment, something I deeply wanted. And once it was fractured and broken, I wanted it even more. Because then, finally, it was familiar. The more he was able to provide better love and caretaking than I'd had in my childhood, the more frightened I became, and the more he subtly put me down and the less he understood why I was scared, the more I thought, "Ah yes, I need more than this. And I know how to operate in a place where I need so much more than I am getting."

So we settled into a place where he came and went, and I waited on the front steps for him to come back again, desperate to do more for him, care more for him, whatever it took to get him to stay. Forget that from the beginning he was ready and willing to stay forever, I couldn't understand that. Someone who just knew he wanted you, forever and always, and was ready and willing to give you what you needed? No, no, let's make this look like something I recognize. Let's ruin everything.

A year later, after a meditation retreat that left me feeling blissed out and forgiving, I emailed him saying that I forgave him. In a lot of ways, though, I do not.

I have spent the years since romanticizing him for the most superficial reasons possible, going back and forth between blaming myself for letting such a "great guy" go, and hating him for being so careless with someone who once meant so much to him. One flaw in my makeup, perhaps—though I don't really see it as one—is that once you've meant something to me, you're in my heart forever. Even if we dated for only a few months, if those months forged a deep closeness, however fleeting, even if you eviscerated me in the end, I would still pick up the phone if you needed me. Because we meant something to each other once. And it confuses me and breaks my heart that no one else seems to think like that. If I have ever loved someone on any level, in a way I always will. And I expect, perhaps naively, that those people will always care about me. I have absolutely thought, during my lowest points, about my exes who were everything to me and wondered if reaching out to them would help, looking for the cure in the cause of the disease.

SO YOUR FAMILY DICTATES YOUR ROMANTIC FUTURE? WHAT A FUN PUNISHMENT!

We are not born knowing how to love anyone, either ourselves or somebody else. However, we are born able to respond to care. . . . Whether we learn how to love ourselves and others will depend on the presence of a loving environment.

—BELL HOOKS, *ALL ABOUT LOVE*

I've internalized so many of the messages we've all been fed about how much your family and your childhood dictate the love you receive as an adult. People will say, "You'll attract someone like your parents," so if you have great parents who are loving and in love, yay, you win! But if you have absent parents or you never knew your parents or your parents were abusive, do you attract ghosts or no one or abusers? Because that seems unfair as hell. You already suffered through not having that baseline of love and support and now you're just screwed and will never experience it because you were born into the wrong place? What the shit, life? Not cool. Or people who say,

"No one will ever love you as much as your mom," which might be comforting to people who have great moms but is a powerfully harmful statement for literally everyone else. So if your mom didn't exist or didn't or couldn't love you, you will never be loved? AWESOME. Great. Just what every unloved little kid wants to hear: Remember how you weren't loved as a kid? Now you'll stay that way until you die!!!

This also goes for "Date a man who loves his mom," or "Date someone who comes from a good family." Because I know what you're trying to say and I do look for both of those things in a partner, based on my background and the idea that I need someone with a stable attachment style, so that one of us is consistently chill. But it also breaks my heart that we tell people this. What is a good family? Is it money? Because we had a lot of that for a little while, but my home life was anything but good. Is it having parents who are still married? Because hahahaha. I have known so many people who come from very wealthy families and/or whose parents are still together, but twist! No one knows how to love, no one hugs each other, maybe one of them is abusive, everyone's in therapy, and they all keep their feelings to themselves. So is that family a good family and mine isn't? I don't think so at all. Or what about a family who is very poor, but so kind and loving and tight-knit? Is that a good family? Better still, I know so many people who came from stereotypically Good Families but are Bad Partners. We have to erase the idea that if you come from anything less than a Good Family, you are bad. And if you come from a Good Family, you're good. But we put this bullshit on one another all the time. Everything, culturally, is weighted by whatever you were born into.

This also always pops into my mind when my female friends will tell me they had a hell of a time with dating, but now they're married or getting married or whatever, so don't worry, it can happen to you!

And whenever they say this, I always ask, "Are you close with your family?" More often than not, they say something like, "Of course. So close," and I'm so confused. Like, wait, you know what love looks like, you grew up with self-esteem and watching parents who loved each other and supported each other and communicated with each other, you had that model, so why did you date turds for seven years before your fiancé? How did you and I both land here? But more important, don't act like you're shocked you're getting married now.

I know this is probably unfair, but it's hard not to feel like, "Of course you found love eventually. If you can see it, you can be it, and all that. You saw love, you grew up with love, you have love all around you, you know you deserve it, you can both receive and give it, so sorry if I'm not totally floored you had a happy ending." But what about the rest of us? Do we get one? I haven't seen much evidence that we do, and it just bums me out.

We put so much weight on the influence of our parents on our psyches, like everything we get in life is luck of the draw, and if you get less-than-ideal parents, welcome to hell! The way we talk about it, it's like a death sentence. Like we all had one shot when we were in utero, and we blew it, no take-backs. But there are also so many inconsistencies in the credit we give to our parents for how we turned out.

Every now and then, I've had someone smile and tell me, "Someone definitely raised you right." And I'll get, without even thinking, very defensive, and reflexively respond, "Actually, I raised myself, so I guess that's also true!" And then it's awkward as fuck and I wish I'd said nothing, and then they feel awkward because wait, what is happening? This got dark fast. To get out of this hole, they'll reply, "Well, you turned out great," almost as if to say, "Well, they couldn't have been that bad if they raised you!" And I'll sigh, because why do we give parents credit for their children automatically?

Surely some kids who became murderers or rapists had pretty A-plus parents—so why did they become murderers and rapists? Maybe they were molested or abused by someone outside the family, or maybe that person was born a straight-up psychopath. We don't know. But in our culture, if anything happens to you as an adult, good or bad, we assume it's your parents' achievement or fault. And obviously there's just no way that's consistently true.

At times I've struggled to feel seen, to have my history feel seen, to have where I come from feel seen because I "turned out great." But that doesn't mean that I Am Fine. I am working every day, tirelessly, like you wouldn't believe, on being fine, fucking finally, can we get this over with, I'm so tired and I just want to travel and eat and smile and move through the world with a semblance of peace.

Still, it is very commonplace for abusive or absent parents, once their (technical) child grows up and becomes successful, to suddenly become Proud Parents! Because they know they can claim you as Theirs now and everyone will believe them. You're like a basic black suitcase that's been circling the baggage claim for twenty-five years and they didn't want you, sneered at what a piece of shit you were, laughed at the idea anyone would have a suitcase that ugly, maybe even kicked you a few times, who knows why, but then the zipper pulled apart and, oh shit, are there diamonds in there? "Excuse me! That's my suitcase! Yeah, totally was this whole time!" It will never occur to these people that you became the person you became *despite* them. That you, magical, wonderful, holy shit wow you, took the bag of rotting maggots they gave you and turned it into Disneyland. That you took years of physical, verbal, and/or sexual abuse, neglect, being told you were worthless, being told you were nothing, shown you were nothing, treated like nothing, and somehow, in your own way, you became everything. And our culture lets them swoop in and claim, "Yeah, my kid's great," and our brains think, "Wow, this person with a great child must also be great!" because we're trained to all the time.

I was recently at the post office and saw a card that read, "Good moms create great kids," and almost flipped all of them around in an attempt to spare anyone else who hates seeing that oversimplified shit when they're just trying to mail an eBay package.

I know people who say "Someone great must've raised you" mean it as a compliment. And I know I am grateful every day I didn't end up living on the street (I don't wanna brag, but I lived in a *car*, so it's like a Days Inn versus a Super 8), or addicted to drugs or alcohol, or other scenarios I don't even want to imagine. But hearing someone speak about all I've achieved, or the person I've become, as though it's the result of a magic wand, or assumed parental support, feels insulting. I made choices no one should have to make, and I still struggle with so many things, so every now and again, I almost wish I hadn't turned out great.

I'm so glad I am where I'm at and am who I am, but it's tough because it can seem like a case of "all's well that ends well," and it is not. And sometimes people's assertion that "Well, you turned out great" can feel like an erasure of my whole life, an erasure of my deliberately turning right when my life veered me left, and keeping my hand on the wheel with everything I had. And I wish people were able to be more nuanced in their response. Maybe an "I'm so proud of you for turning out great anyway," like it's an achievement, far from inevitable, rare and indicative of courage. Or a "Wow, then it's even more impressive, by miles, that you're as incredible as you are now. You should be very proud of how you turned out." Just to give people who have lived through hell, with little to no help from the usual suspects, if nothing else, the ownership and credit for the magic they alone created from absolutely nothing.

So if you raised yourself, and you're reading this, I am so proud of you. You raised a hell of a kid. And it wasn't easy—I can't even imagine, no one can. (Okay, I kind of can, but still.) But you're here and you could've easily backslid into pain and nothingness and worthlessness and hopelessness, and maybe you did backslide, time and again, but every time, you climbed back up and tried to be kinder and softer and find more room in your heart for compassion instead of hatred, hope instead of defeat. And let me tell you, someone (you) really raised you right.

BABIES BABYSITTING BABIES

You were born into a family that doesn't always appreciate
you. But one day things are going to be very different.

—MISS HONEY, *MATILDA*

I started babysitting at around ten years old—you know, the age
when a child still needs a babysitter herself. As I saw it, I was already
raising myself and my sister, and you know what would be a fun
home to be in as much as possible? Not my home! Add in the fact
that as far back as I can remember, I'd gotten the distinct impression
my parents were not exactly in this for the long haul. I can't really
remember a time when I didn't think I needed to start earning money
so I could support myself.

I also knew I was going to be a comedian/writer/actor/musician,
and those people don't usually make a ton of money right off the bat,
so I figured why not combine my blossoming childhood work addic-
tion with my desperate need to feel like I'll be able to support myself
in a few years so I don't end up homeless and die, which is everyone's
primary childhood fear! My recently proven track record of being

very, very good at child care led to my early career in babysitting. (Hi, again, I'm ten in this story.)

Because it was a small town, I babysat for the woman who lived down the street, Mrs. Anders. Mrs. Anders was very quick to tell me during my Job Interview—ten, I'm ten—that they didn't live in this development, no, no, they were just here for a few months while their much larger, better house was being built, making me feel incredibly poor in a weirdly adult way. Her husband owned a large, high-end jewelry store in the area that I had heard of, as it bore their name: Anders Jewelry. (I just quickly googled them; they do not have a very high Yelp rating, which makes me feel better about this sad woman politely letting me know she was richer than me, which honestly, the more I think about it, Jesus, she must have been such a sad lady to have to brag about having a fancy house to a freaking child she was hiring to take care of her children. I'm sorry for your wealthy sadness, Mrs. Anders. I hope you're divorced now and live in the woods and make jam every day and your hair is super long and sometimes it gets caught in the jam and you laugh.)

I don't want to brag, but I nailed the interview, having spent most of my childhood auditioning for pretty much everyone all the time. "Adopt me! Hear that I can really, really sing, I can! Please protect me, things aren't great at home!" I had become very, very skilled at being poised and witty and very adult. Being a child is so lonely in and of itself, even without added abuse and neglect and fear for your own life and the lives of everyone around you; merging the two can create a powder keg of need that quickly solidified my one huge goal: to work all the time, in every possible way, and to be perfect. To be so perfect they had to hire me, had to notice me, had to see me, had to love me, had to take care of me.

Around this time, I remember taking care of Mrs. Anders's two-year-old girl and being silly and sweet with her, and taking care of the baby girl while I was watching TV, letting myself fall into the constant commercials for Anders Furniture and imagining where they would move soon—betcha he reads, betcha she sews, maybe she's made me a closet of clothes, etc.—and thinking maybe if I was a good enough babysitter, they'd take me with them. But also, no, because who would take care of my sister, never mind.

I babysat until I was about fourteen years old—you know, the age when you usually *start* babysitting. Not me—that was my retirement age. That's when I started cleaning houses, as many as possible, and working every other odd job I could, sometimes five at a time, gotta pay these future bills, man! Gotta pay 'em! I'd clean weird houses in the neighborhood and they'd leave for a few hours and I'd blast alternative radio and use the time as a great reason to practice my singing while "dusting the moldings" like Ms. IDontRememberHerName-ButSheWasNotSuperNice asked. I so clearly remember dusting while getting deeply into the maudlin joy of belting Sheryl Crow's "My Favorite Mistake" and "Strong Enough" loudly enough to fill the whole house until I could hear myself really clearly and think, "Wow. I'm getting really good. Nice." And then back to scrubbing the floors.

I can't count how many families I've babysat for, but I definitely picked it back up after high school, continuing swiftly along my workaholic path. By the time I got to New York City, though, it was different. After you're out of high school and are more formally in your adult years, you notice more. You notice the parents who don't hug their kids. You notice the parents who hate their partner and it permeates every inch of the home, no matter how spacious or well decorated. You notice the mom who keeps you for an extra two hours after each ten-hour shift, whether you want to stay or not, so she can bitch about her husband while she pays you ten dollars an hour—

cheaper than therapy for her—which makes you resent her, but you also understand this role and you keep quiet as the anger builds. You notice your wanting to take these kids and to love them forever in a way their parents can't or won't. You notice all the parents reluctant to pick their kids up from school. It's not as if they're bad people, but you feel their "ugh, gotta take care of these dicks" resentment, which might actually be a very understandable level of exhaustion backed by so much love, but nevertheless, you hear it and you're a child again. An act of emotional transference occurs, and suddenly they're your family and you're the child they wish would go away but won't. And you see those little kids who are not you, but seem to feel how you felt, and you would do anything to protect them.

I remember one job interview for a family like this and the mom told me, "Yeah, FYI, they both have the flu, they've had it for like three weeks now." I, appalled, said, "Have you given them anything for it?" and she said, "We had steak last night." I said, "I mean, like, medicine, vitamins . . ." and she said, "I don't know. There's some expensive Whole Foods vitamins in the fridge, but I haven't tried that." Five seconds later I literally begged her to hire me because this was so upsetting.

I could talk about the rich, bizarre worlds I lived in while babysitting, about Samantha, a two-year-old who was spunky and too loud and too weird for her parents, who would sing at the mailman with me (songs about spaceships, duh), and cried when girls her age (they're mean at two?????) wouldn't play with her and so we went elsewhere together and blew bubbles and I told her I liked her so much more than all those girls combined and that one good person who loves you is always way better than three mean ones who don't, and she nodded and I smiled and she laughed and we ate golden raisins and it felt better.

Or about Amelia, who was friends with the other girls I was babysitting, but we spent all our time together on the playground. Amelia was seven and had a tiny mustache above her upper lip and bushy black eyebrows and we met because she told me she liked my style. I was wearing rainbow knee socks and heart stickers on my cheeks and a dress with flowers on it and glitter rings on my hands, which had hearts drawn on them in Sharpie—eternally a children's TV host (or, as some drunk people on the train recently described me, "OMG, you look like Zenon: Girl of the 21st Century," which is fair. I will also gladly accept that I look like a human My Little Pony or Rainbow Brite, all style icons obviously). Amelia had too many feelings and a huge imagination and no one liked her and I didn't get it! "This kid has it all!!!! Cool ideas! Mismatched socks! An Amélie haircut! A sick mustache! WHAT ARE YOU NOT GETTING, FELLOW YOUTHS????" Fuckin' idiots. Amelia ruled. We started scheduling playdates with Amelia's sister, who was "cooler" (pfft), and the girls I babysat for, specifically because I wanted to be Amelia's friend so bad. I wanted to hear her British accents and tell her they were so, so good and to play video games with her and make up silly voices for the characters and, when she felt too many feelings, raise her chin with my hand and tell her, "Hey, that is what makes you *great.*"

Subconsciously, I thought if I couldn't find the person I'd been waiting my whole life for, I'd be that person for other people. If I couldn't have parents, I'd be everyone else's parents. If no one was going to take care of me, I would take care of everyone. If no one was going to tell me all the things I'd always wanted to hear, I'd make damn sure as many people on earth as possible heard them. So at least someone was.

My last two babysitting jobs were my favorite. One was a six-year-old girl named Rhiannon who was so stunning that everywhere we went, because often people assume any woman with any child is their mom, people would tell me my daughter was gorgeous and should be a model. Now, first of all, I would think, "I AM NOT HER FUCKING MOMMMMMM. DO I LOOK OLD ENOUGH TO BE A MOM? NO!!!!! GOOD DAY!" but then I would think, "Oh man, you think I'd make kids this pretty? That's sick. Thanks, dude." Finally, I'd land on ushering her out of there and remind her she was tough and strong, so she wouldn't become like one of the many women in the world who are often (and exclusively) told they're pretty pretty pretty until everything else they are (which is a lot) fades out of focus and doesn't matter and so they lean into it with all they have. They're the Pretty Girl. Don't let your intelligence steal focus, don't be too witty, don't be too intimidating or have too much to say. Just be pretty forever. And by forever we mean like five to ten years, because then it ends and you better have gotten married by then, because otherwise you're dead, it's over. And I am fucking done with this happening to women. I am beyond done.

I took every chance I could get to remind her she wasn't just, as she told me, "maybe kind of braver than the boys in my class, because I jump off that high beam all the time and they won't even try! But I don't know." I'd tell her she did know, that she was braver and so strong and so smart and so kind. I hoped that for every "you're so pretty" compliment she received, I could make up for it with twenty "you're superstrong, dudes!" and a high five.

The other was an eight-year-old boy named Phoenix, who was described to me on the phone by his mom as "a very sensitive little boy, he's small for his age, he has a lot of food allergies, and he loves art, especially the color pink." If I could've jumped through the phone to start the job at the end of that sentence, I would've. When I met Phoenix, we were both a little cagey and acted different than we were.

But what we were was so painfully similar. After a few months, once our walls had dropped, we'd spend hours hosting a fake TV show we created (and hosted) called *Deadly Waters*. *Deadly Waters* was a show about the deadliest of deadly liquids that were super deadly. So we'd take ketchup and mustard and pickle juice and turmeric and sugar and honey and anything else we could find, and mix it in a glass and then tell our viewers why this liquid was the deadliest deadly liquid in the history of deadlies, and just how many people's lives it had already claimed, which was always in the millions. He'd watch magic shows on his iPad and I'd try to find a way to remind him that it was super weird and dumb that women were always assistants in bikinis, with no lines, and he'd agree it was. One day he drew a photo where he was the magician and I was a magician too and we both wore our normal clothes and got the same lines and it made my whole day.

His parents had told me when I was hired that they liked to sing to Phoenix before he went to sleep and they had a book of songs they kept under his bed if you needed to look at lyrics and if I wouldn't mind. Uh, OF COURSE I WOULDN'T MIND, SINGING IS MY LIFE. So five nights a week, I would head upstairs with him and read him stories and pick three songs out of the book, but after a while I'd rely on a few go-tos to sing to him: Fleetwood Mac's "Storms," Nina Simone's "I Shall Be Released," Leonard Cohen's "Hallelujah," the Beatles's "All My Loving" and "Real Love," and anything soft and soothing that I could also really fucking nail. One day, after I started singing to him every night, his mom said, "Phoenix says you have a beautiful voice!" to which he said, "Mooooom!!!!" like I wasn't sup-posed to know that!!! And I told them I was, um, also a comedian and musician, so like, uh, yeah. Phoenix's eyes got huge, and the more I showed him YouTube clips online or press pieces in the paper, the more he thought I was magic and would tell anyone who came by:

"My babysitter is a comedian! And she's in a band!" Even thinking of it now makes me cry.

His mom once told me his past babysitters had tried to hug him, but he didn't like it when they did, so please do not be offended that he hates hugs. But every time I'd come to the door, he'd run to open it and jump into my arms. Kids know.

I babysat him for several wonderful, wonderful years that, once we hit a stride, made it hard to give up. So much so that when I got offered a job as sex and relationships editor at *Cosmopolitan*, I remember telling my roommate, "And I'd get out at like six, so if I wanted to still keep my babysitting job, I could!" and he looked at me like I was nuts. "You just got a job doing what you actually want to be doing, that pays more than the, like, hundred dollars a week you've been making and you're worried how you're going to keep both?" I shot him a look, like, "Uh, YEAH!"

Phoenix was Jewish and adorably proudly so, and he asked his parents if I could spend Hanukkah with them and watch him light the candles, and I think it started to feel like I had a family, because he made me part of his. One day, while walking home from school, I asked him if he'd ever baked Christmas cookies and he told me no and I said, "What???" and he said, "Lane, I'm Jewish!" and I said "Okay, then they're Hanukkah cookies! They can be whatever you want, dude. Let's do it! You want to?" and he said, "Okay!" I bought allergy-free cookie mix and then we swung by the toy store on the way home.

While we walked down the aisles, I wandered into aisle four, which was like a pink explosion with dolls and pink pink pink everywhere. I'd forgotten how gendered toy stores are: pink pink pink and sparkles and glitter, and then blue and gray and metal and plastic. Phoenix had not forgotten. I watched him pass the aisles looking for me, seeing I was in the pink toy aisle, thought about walking down, and then, as if a trip wire would strangle him if he walked any farther, walked past the aisle and onto the next.

I went to the next aisle to find him and said, "Hey. What's up? Did you wanna look down there?" and he said, tightly, fists clenched, jaw tight, "Noooo!" "Why not?" "That's the . . . pink toy aisle." As though "pink toy" was street slang and I knew what he meant, everyone knew! I did know, but I pressed anyway. "So? You like pink. We color with pink all the time." "I know, but it's different!" he said, jaw still tight, voice still hushed. "How is it different?" "It just is!!!!" he said, seeming like he might cry. I took him over to the aisle and said, "Look, there's a cash register. You love playing store, right?" He wouldn't even look at it and said, "Can we go, please?"

He was eight, and he'd already been taught that there was nearly nothing as shameful or disgusting, or whisper-quiet-inappropriate, as liking something feminine. And it broke my heart—for him, and for all the boys I know as adults who were softer, more sensitive, more expressive, more open when they were little and then were told to shut all that down. And we wonder why we have grown men at odds with their female partners who are begging them to be more open, to share their feelings, to be softer, to be sweeter, to be gentler, and they just can't do it. They'd spent their childhoods having people tell them to be the opposite of all of those things, to kill that part of them until there was nothing left—and they did that, just like everyone asked, but now the world wants them to be like that again, and they just can't. It's a heartbreaking loss for everyone. I wanted, more than anything, to help Phoenix keep the things he would need, the things we *all* need, later in life.

On the way home, I struggled with what to say. We turned onto his block and I just said, "You can like anything you want, okay? If you like princess stuff, that's so cool, dude. If you like pink, pink is a great color and you'd look awesome in it. If you wanna put glitter on your cheeks, I do it all the time! I could give you some of mine." He just looked at the ground. I got on the ground and just said, "You don't have to do anything, ever. But you can also do everything, if you want to." And we went inside to bake cookies.

While we folded the dough together and sang along to sixties music on the radio, he turned to me and said, "Lane, can we do this every year together?" and I just thought, "Aww, you think things last." I knew I probably wouldn't work there in a year, let alone every year. I had a hunch that this was a stopping point before the big show, the last job I'd have that was just to pay my rent while I did what I loved on the side. And it was.

When I gave my notice, I told them they should still let me know if they ever needed anyone on weekends or something, but as I got busier and busier, they called less, probably assuming I was too busy and wouldn't want to. But I always wanted to. Will always want to.

In the last few months of my time with Pheonix, our time together got shorter. His parents' schedules were different and they didn't need me as much, so I had maybe only three hours with him two days a week, and it wasn't enough. On those days, Phoenix would, without fail, let me in the door, hug me with everything he had, and we'd eat snacks and watch TV on opposite sides of the couch for about two hours. Also without fail, about ten minutes before it was time to go upstairs to bed, Phoenix would scoot over to my side of the couch to put his head in my lap and I'd brush his hair back while we watched TV. And then it was time to go to bed. And every time he'd be so sad we had to go to bed already, but really, sad that he'd just gotten the courage to reach out, to get closer, to lie in my lap like he'd wanted to, to dare to be needy, and I'd gladly accepted, and it was already over. And it was the most relatable thing to witness.

How many times I've sat with people, even as an adult, wishing I could hold their hand, or lie in their lap, or cry in front of them, or tell them how I really felt about them, or ask them how they really felt about me, and how many hours I wasted thinking of how I would do it, when I should do it, begging myself to "just do it now! Who cares!" Then once I did it, I'd wish I'd done it so much sooner because it was fine, it was safe, I was safe.

So one night when his mom came home I told her, "I noticed Phoenix is doing this thing where we'll sit apart for hours and then he'll finally get up the courage to come lie in my lap, when time is almost up. And I would just offer to have him come cuddle with me, but I don't want him to feel like he has to. Is there a way I could come over a little earlier so maybe he can have more time to get up the courage to ask?" She looked at me sweetly and said, "Of course."

The next night, right on schedule, he got up the courage to come lie in my lap and I brushed his hair back while we watched *Myth-Busters*, and magically, it wasn't time to go to bed just yet, and I think he noticed. Because he looked up at me and smiled. Like he knew.

"JUST A FEW NOTES FOR OUR NEW BABYSITTER!"

(Previously published in *The New Yorker*'s Shouts and Murmurs column. Author's note: I've worked for some incredible families and this story is purely comedic fiction and exaggerated based on some less than ideal families I have worked with. To the great families I worked for, this is not about you.)

Welcome! We've interviewed *so* many babysitters who didn't really have what we were looking for, but then we realized that if we didn't lower our standards we wouldn't have anyone—and here you are! Anyway, let me give you a little tour before I introduce you to Brick.

I hope our house wasn't too hard to find. I know you're poorer than we are, so you probably aren't in this neighborhood that often. We moved here years ago, when we still made way more money than you do, but the point is to keep reminding you that we're not *that* rich. We're not. We're really not. Did you park outside? Oh, it's a bike! But that's nice. You're having fun. God, I miss being young and poor.

You can put your quirky tote bag on top of our quirky tote bags that cost significantly more than yours. You'll probably never see it again, but I doubt you'll miss your two dollars and that MetroCard that doesn't swipe.

So this is the living room we never spend any time in, but, gosh, doesn't it give the impression that nothing bad ever happens here? And it didn't, until 2013, so that's good.

This is the kitchen where my borderline-eating-disorder-masked-as-health-consciousness is laid bare as new-fallen snow. Oh, that shelf that's just vitamins? Those aren't for Brick. They're to supplement my daily diet of a thimble of avocado spread on a rice cake. Rice cakes are in the cupboard, by the way. Feel free to eat anything you want because the more you eat, the less food there is in the house when my stomach turns into a fist that punches me awake in the night and I go to scarf down a whole can of pumpkin puree.

And if you ever want some water or juice, it's in the fridge, but please consume only one glass of it while you're here. I'll never tell you why, but if you take any more than that I'll keep you for two hours after work to complain about how I think my husband is having an affair as I chain-smoke the cigarettes I keep in the freezer.

There he is! This is Brick. Brick is the sweetest, most entitled yet also neglected child you'd ever want to meet. He's incredibly loving, but be warned: He hates hugs, which is why I don't give him any. Or I never hug him, so he hates hugs? I'm not sure, but either way . . . Hold on, I just got a text.

Sorry, that was my husband. He once dreamed of being an artist, but now he's a lawyer and blames me for crushing his spirit. But as I tell him, "Look, the money for Brick's aerial dance classes has to come from somewhere, and it certainly isn't going to be from your oil paintings of the *Friends* coffee shop."

I'll let you and Brick have some playtime while I go take the towels out of the dryer and bury my face in one and scream into it. He loves Legos!

In terms of the schedule, I'll typically need you five times a week between 3:00 and 4:15 p.m., and then again from 4:45 to 6:49. What happens between 4:15 and 4:45 is none of your concern, and I will not be paying you for that half hour. During that time, you're more than welcome to stare at our wall of family photos that were all taken the year Brick was born. They will probably make you wonder how such a seemingly loving family could go from weekends at the lake to setting up online dating profiles just to see what's out there. At 4:45, it'll be time for Brick's snack.

I can't think of anything else you need to know right now, but really, most of this you'll pick up just by spending time with our son, who will lean on you for the emotional support that no one else in this family seems capable of providing. I'm personally excited that I'll have someone to treat both like a close friend and a housekeeper while paying you as little as possible, and I'm sure my husband will be very excited that you're young enough for him to "jokingly" hit on in a way that will make you feel uncomfortable. But more than anything, Brick is so excited you're here that he's already stolen the contents of your tote while we've been sitting here talking. He truly is a genius, though you will never see any evidence of that and will spend most of your time wondering how young is too young to be considered a sociopath.

Brick previously had a wonderful nanny named Imogen who unfortunately left us to go pursue her dream of not being a babysitter. We all miss her, but, honestly, if I could run away from this family, I would too.

AM I THE LAST HOPELESS ROMANTIC ON EARTH?

I have this dream of being whole.
Of not going to sleep each night, wanting.
But still sometimes, when the wind is warm
or the crickets sing . . . I dream of a love
that even time will lie down and be still for.

—SALLY OWENS, *PRACTICAL MAGIC*

I first started having what most people would probably consider casual sex (sex without our technically being "together," though to be honest, I don't think it ever felt totally casual by any means because I can't pull that off) after the breakup with Everett that I couldn't shake, probably because the breakup seemingly lasted for centuries. From what I'd heard, casual sex would be a good way to shake it. I remember thinking it was really cool that all these people wanted to sleep with me and that we could sleep together—just sex, no strings attached, just like in the movies!

And it was the worst. I'd gone from having this relationship with someone I was crazy, stupid in love with to having mediocre sex with people I hardly knew, hardly cared about, who hardly knew and hardly cared about me. It felt hollow and sad every time. But I kept trying to make myself do this thing I thought I was supposed to do, trying it on for size, even though it never, ever fit me.

So I ignored the gut-punch I would feel every time I got out of the bed of someone whom I didn't really want to be with, or whom I thought maybe it'd be nice to be with but we "weren't labeling it." I turned off parts of my heart and brain, which are two of my favorite—and most vital—parts of myself.

And then one day I was just done with pretending I was too cool for it. Maybe it was almost throwing up on a girl I almost slept with whom I didn't care about, to the point where my body physically revolted and caused me to nearly puke on her face, maybe not. Either way, I just couldn't do it anymore. It no longer seemed worth it to try to be someone I'm not, especially when I love all the things that I am. I love how intensely I love people, especially despite my background. I think it's an incredible gift to meet people you connect with and want to give all of yourself to, to be able to risk that much of yourself to go all in with someone, because why the fuck not?

I know it's so much cooler to meet someone at a bar and fuck them in a bathroom stall and never speak to that person again, because who cares. And I know people who do that, and I love them to pieces because they're exploring and it's working for them. But I just don't fucking want to hook up with some guy or girl whose jokes aren't that funny, who makes me feel like he or she is not sure about me, and who won't give me a straight answer about what we are to each other, when that would make me feel a lot better because I'm a human person with feelings. I don't want to respond to their stupid, half-assed texts that they probably send me while they're crapping. I don't want to come to your place for a "chill hang sesh," or hear you call me your "friend" when we've had our faces on each other's junk. But I had friends telling me this was what you do, this is what dating is, stop expecting more, and honestly, I'm just so fucking over people telling me the right way to do things. And let me tell you, people love telling single people the right way to do things.

If you've ever been the Single Friend who complained about how everyone sucks and no one is worth dating, you've had at least one (if not, like, four hundred) coupled friends telling you, "Stop looking! That's when love finds you." And if you're like me, you want to go over to that person's house and knock everything off their shelves for sport. I get what they're saying: they're trying to tell me not to focus on it like this goal I have to achieve or else my body will explode, and that's solid advice. But telling people who understandably want to find love and happiness that they can find those things only if they erase them from their brain is fucking dumb for so many reasons.

Telling yourself not to look for love is like telling yourself not to look for food or air or water or clothes that fit you perfectly. Sure, maybe those things will find you, but since they're all wonderful, you probably want to really put in the effort to find them. But here's the thing: Implementing a strategy on how to find love, even if that strategy is to not look for it, IS STILL LOOKING FOR IT.

So now you're off on a quest to let the world know, "I am not looking for love (but by my saying that, I totally am, FYI)," which is just as much of a plan as making a secret Pinterest board for your future wedding while you're single.

Telling people who actively want to find love that they should stop wanting to find love so they *can* find love is like telling a depressed person they can be happy only once they don't want to be happy. What the shit is that? It makes zero sense.

Again, I get it, I'm not an idiot; I know what they mean. In general, it's great if people can just focus on who they are and making themselves happy and learning to be happy alone. Those are all great pieces of advice, but they're also notoriously hard to implement.

Why is love the one thing that you're supposed to just happen upon with zero effort? If you wanted to get a great job, no one would tell you to end your job search and chill in Starbucks until someone tapped you on the shoulder and offered you one. They'd tell you to ask around and put in the time, because that's how you get what you want. What about all of the people who found love *because* they were looking for it? There are tons of people who put out online dating profiles or agreed to a setup or braved a singles mixer and found someone they loved.

We all want love. We do. It's what makes us people with hearts and feelings and access to so many romantic comedies. And sure, maybe some people found love by releasing their need to find it, and that's great. But stop telling people that they need to actively change who they are in order to find love. Because even if you do find love that way, changing yourself to find it means your partner may not have fallen for the real you anyway.

I am ready for meet-cutes at all times. I'm eternally aware of strangers on the street holding hands. I notice everyone's ring finger every time I see them. I get excited when the clock reads 2:14 because that's Valentine's Day!!! My favorite number has always been two. I see hearts in rain puddles and shapes of leaves. I live for the moments when someone is saying something, and there's something about the way their mouth moves or their eyes light up that makes you think, "Man, I love this person." I look for love. I'm proud to admit that I want to find someone incredible to share my life with, and I can't wait to meet them. The worst that could happen if I do all of these things and continue my unrelenting search is I go through life alone, but still living every minute as the romantic weirdo I know I am deep down. And if you're reading this and you're like that too, if it's any consolation, that makes two of us.

Why can't we respond to someone's cute texts right away? Why can't we say yes to dates instead of playing coy? Why can't we sleep with someone as soon as we want to? Because if we do something wrong, we might mess everything up? Nonsense. Whenever I start thinking that way, I remind myself, "If this person is really your soul mate, you can't text them too much or too soon or be too much for them. If it's right, there's nothing you can do wrong."

If you go in fearlessly from the start, yeah, you might get hurt and it might not work out. But at least you really experienced how wonderful it was, for however long it was wonderful. And then, years later, if you're still together, your "We said 'I love you' after three dates" way *was* the right way for you. But you can get to that point only if you trust that what you feel is real, for now at least, and go all in.

But we don't think like this anymore. Guys don't set out to date the girls they want to marry. If anything, I've actually heard the words "I can't date you, you're the girl you marry," which, like, wow, what a backhanded compliment, thank you! I've also heard, "You're third-wife material, like after I've made all my mistakes and realized I want something truly great." Cool, I'll definitely be sure to remain single until I'm sixty and you're single again! Won't move an inch! LMK!

And because we've all been taught guys want girls who are chill and don't "think like that" (yeah, god forbid you want something real and admit that openly), we lower our expectations because, again, we want to be chosen. And in that way, without our even knowing it, it becomes a contest for who can withstand the most. We know trying to change someone won't work, so we've created a work-around for this, which is supporting our partners while they treat us like shit, and being so so patient while they hopefully magically become better people. Which is totally different from trying to change someone! It is! Because obviously trying to change someone is so stupid, haha, for sure. And we're not doing that! We're just providing the emotional labor and the tools and the insight and a place for their pain and rage to go, holding anything they need like an unpaid therapist, so they can magically change on their own. Please. It's the same thing.

And to make things even worse, some couples will tell you that your horribly unhealthy situation is how they met their husband, so now you're putting up with being treated badly and his shutting down and not being ready, because "what if that's your story!!!" And one lady at work said her husband was horrible to her for three years until she nursed him back to health and now they're soul mates. And let me just say, lady at work, keep that shit to yourself. I'm so glad it worked for you, but telling people your exception-to-the-rule story can be dangerous for other people, especially when they're in pain and their story might not work out positively at all. After Everett yelled at me on the phone, I shut down. I couldn't be with anyone who would yell at me and hang up; I thought it was a black-and-white indicator that we weren't compatible. But then someone told me, "Eh, couples fight! People yell. It's fine!" and maybe she's right, but I wish I hadn't listened to her and thrown myself back into dating Everett, who wasn't compatible with me for so many reasons, because I had every right to think, "Yeah, yelling is a dealbreaker for me," even if some random girl felt like yelling was normal and everyone yells, who cares.

But we put up with it for so many reasons. The possibility that our story isn't perfect, that people aren't perfect, that our person is just having a rough patch and it'll smooth out soon, and because, if you're in your late twenties, you're running out of time. We tell people there are specific set-in-stone ages they have to be somebody, find somebody, or else they're fucked, and it'd be cool if that stopped.

When I was a teenager, my dad once told me that "if a woman is thirty and no man has ever proposed to her, there's something wrong with her." I remember thinking, "Yeah, maybe she had you for a dad."

Timelines are bullshit. The whole "your dateability ends at thirty, so you'd better get married" shit was created when we lived to be, like, sixty years old max and you could have babies only until, like, thirty-one. Now people live past a hundred and have babies at forty-six. Why are we still keeping these notions going? To keep people, especially women, scared and settling, eager to marry someone who is good enough for now, this will do, the store's almost closing and it's better than nothing? Just so they can take the next ten years to figure out this is exactly what happened and then they're thirty-eight and divorced and shit, what now? Because you did everything right, you stuck to the timeline, damn the cost, and it should've magically worked out and it didn't.

I see happy couples on the subway now and think warmly, "I've had that," like I'm ninety years old and that was eighty years ago. But it often feels like that's how long it has been since I've met someone truly great who honestly seemed like they could love me properly. Or even simply seemed like they wanted all the old-fashioned rom-com shit I want.

Last winter, a guy emailed me telling me he was hoping he'd show up on my Tinder during Tinder Live, my comedy show where I go on my Tinder account live on stage, which Frank Conniff from *Mystery Science Theater 3000* told me he describes as "like *Mystery Science Theater 3000*, if the movie could talk back," which is the best description. I laughed it off. He later wrote me an email formally stating he was a fan of the show and had a crush on me and knew I was a hopeless romantic and he was too and he'd love to take me on a date sometime. My heart immediately melted like frosting made with coconut oil, which, if you didn't know, is very melty. I often feel like the last hopeless romantic on the entire planet, so meeting another one was like spotting a hot guy at Forever 21. You're kind of like, "Um, what are you doing here? Obviously I'm glad you're here, but also what are you doing here? I thought you were a myth."

Because he'd made the declaration that he was a romantic, as such a small percentage of people seem to be, I innately trusted it. And I looked up his Twitter to see a photo of him and checked out his Instagram and saw that he was actually cute, so I was excited and hopeful that he didn't fall into the common category of "he's hot but his brain sucks and his mouth's not good." (Seriously, if I could use "find and replace" on my exes, I'd erase almost all of them. Unrelated, I also think Napchat is a good idea for an app. It'd basically just be a place to co-nap with friends so you can wake up together, like, "Oh, hey, what's up?")

So later when I agreed to a date and he asked me about all of the things I liked to do and said he would make a plan (!!!) for us based on that, I was ecstatic. He asked me for a list of things I loved and then said he'd spend the week thinking of some elaborate, wonderful thing for us to do together.

Later, when the plan (which was delivered to me three hours before we were supposed to meet up) turned out to be "Yeah, I couldn't think of anything. You just wanna walk around in the blizzard outside?" my face dropped and I threw my phone into a nearby toilet. (Not really, because phones are expensive, but in my mind it happened.) And this man told me he was a hopeless romantic! I'd finally found one and he still thought this was good??? Listen, you can date however you want to, but come on, you claim you're a romantic and wanna take me for a great night and then you treat me like a blind date from Craigslist with feet for hands?

Am I the last remaining hopeless romantic in the world? I'm nearly certain I can't be, and it's very likely you're reading this, going, "Me! I am too!" And if that's the case, I would hug you for eternity if I could because it is not a chill way to be right now.

Most of the time, whenever I tell men I'm a hopeless romantic, they look at me the same way they do when I tell them I have food allergies: It's not a dealbreaker, but they'd rather it wasn't a thing. And you know what? Me too, in both cases!

I swear there were years of my life when I dated guys who brought me flowers every time they saw me and sent me love letters in the mail and wrote poetry. Or drew me as a cool little cartoon or took me to this incredibly romantic out-of-the-way spot so we could sit there and look at the stars and trees and feel like we were inside a rom-com. And then at some point, things changed. My hunch is, as soon as "Netflix and chill" became an option, a lot of guys were, like, "Whoa, we don't have to put in any effort at all? Rad." And we went along with it in an attempt to be Chill Girls who didn't need all that stuff anyway.

But for some of us, um, we still need them, and not having them is increasingly feeling like a freaking rip-off. To those who think you don't want these things, I point to: literally all TV/movies/music. So you mean to tell me you can watch the early seasons of *The Office* and be, like, "Eh, what Jim and Pam have is amazing, but I'd prefer drinking bad beers on a couch until he touches my boobs and then says, 'Let's hang again next week?' Really? If so, that's totally okay, but if not, and you're feeling like "Wait, we still have romance in TV and movies and music, but not in our real dating lives? WTF?" Then hello, welcome, grab a seat.

I don't know when a date went from a beautiful, elaborately planned evening designed to steal your heart and prove how much they liked you to "You wanna come chill on my roof?" because that lazy bullshit is not working for me.

Why did we stop wanting dinner and a movie and maybe flowers, because why not flowers?! When did we stop thinking that courtship was too time consuming and everything romantic comedies waxed on about was just a dumb fairy-tale concept, instead of our expectation for romantic love?

I'm tired of pretending I'm cool with whatevs. I'm tired of pretending that laziness can replace thoughtfulness and still be acceptable to me. I want it all, man. I want someone who asks me out to make an actual plan, whether that plan involves a jet or a stack of nickels (money is not the issue here), then picks me up at my house and takes me on an actual date full of adorable surprises, not for any kind of financial display necessarily, but because they want me to know that they know I'm special and worth it. I want sweetly curated Spotify playlists and texts in the middle of the day that say cheesy shit like "Hi, I miss you and you're gorgeous and very smart and have a lot of nice jeans, bye." I want someone who will be the kind of boyfriend my friends will describe as "Oh my god, he's like a human version of *The Notebook*," instead of as "the guy who asked you to chill on his roof at eleven p.m. and who frankly scares us."

A few months ago, another guy asked me out; then, on the day of what would've been our date, he said, "Let's just figure something out." Which sounded like "Maybe we can have a drink and you'll decide if light groping in a back room is a kind of date." And my romantic self said, "Enough."

I told him that we could go out when he had a plan. He never rose to that hilariously simple and reasonable request, and it felt not only fine but good. Because I hadn't sat passively, hoping he'd become someone he never indicated he could be. And sure, you could argue that I could've made the plans, but I've done that for so many years and I don't want to. It's as simple as that! It's not a gender thing, but I want to be courted. I want to be swept off my feet, to be impressed. I want to be bowled over with how romantic someone is and how much they want to make my night and my life more special and incredible and phenomenal than it was before they entered it.

And I know, I can feel it in my bones that this person is out there for me, and for you if that's what you truly want.

And they will make all our exes look like fucking jokes.

TV COUPLES WHO MADE ME BELIEVE LOVE IS SUPPOSED TO BE BETTER THAN THIS

For a really long time that's all I had. I just had little
moments with a girl who saw me as a friend. And
a lot of people told me I was crazy to wait this long
for a date with a girl who I worked with, but I think
even then I knew that I was waiting for my wife.

—JIM HALPERT, *THE OFFICE*

It will not at all surprise you to know that a lifelong hopeless romantic with an overactive imagination and a not-that-great personal life who loves TV has shipper tendencies (see: someone who gets incredibly passionate about a fictional relationship, be it TV or film or in books, what have you). Mine range from Logan in *Veronica Mars* (I know he's not perfect, but they're Logan and Veronica, what do you want from me), Leslie and Ben from *Parks and Recreation* (the best TV couple to ever exist), Olive and Todd from *Easy A*, Chris and Jal and Freddie and Effy from *Skins*, Jane Villanueva and Rafael Solano from *Jane the Virgin* (I know Michael Cordero was her heart, but have you seen Rafael? Have you?), Idgie and Ruth from *Fried Green Tomatoes*, Jim Halpert and Pam Beesly from *The Office* (seasons one through four only), Gunnar and Scarlett from *Nashville* (seasons one through four only), and Jaye and Eric from *Wonderfalls*. I have at times thought of making my Tinder bio "Jim Halpert or die."

And yes, I do watch these shows over and over again, often curating specific episodes like "Okay, so we should start here because this is when Ben and Leslie first meet," like I'm creating a super-cut version of the show that plays out like a twenty-hour rom-com. And even though that's a fucking long rom-com, I am always so gutted when TV shows end, when a TV rewatch is done. Often I'll go back and start the whole thing over again because I don't want to leave that world. I want to stay safely wrapped inside it, so immersed I feel like I can move within that world, that I live inside it, that I'm a part of it. Nik once very accurately observed about my obsessive relationship with television: "Oh my god, Lane. I just realized something. You rewatch your favorite shows because they're like your family. The characters are people who are there for you when you need them, you've grown to love them, you know them well, you've spent so much time with them. In some cases, the shows were with you when you were growing up, they raised you, they're your family. And when they're done, you don't want them to leave because then you're alone again and your family is gone." And he was very, very correct.

But back to Jim Halpert.

Before I first started watching the American version of *The Office*, I remember my friend Joy telling me, "Jim Halpert is like porn for female writers," and then later watching the show and thinking, "Truer words were never spoken, my friend Joy."

In the years since, I have come to the conclusion that Jim Halpert probably doesn't exist. Like, I want him to exist more than anything so we can get married ASAP literally anywhere at all. In a ditch? Sure. Outside a gas station? Okay. On a stranger's porch until they ask us to leave? Fine. But in my experience, Jim Halpert is as unattainable of an ideal as you can get because he makes even the most well-meaning dudes look like serial killer bores and I hate it.

I seriously can't watch seasons one through three of *The Office* without just crying nonstop at how beautiful the world would be if more dudes were Jim Halpert in pretty much all of the ways. It's physically painful to behold his existence, and I don't feel like that's an exaggeration. His relationship with Pam is basically a fairy tale that seems like it could actually happen, so once you get out into the world of online dating apps and guys you meet at bars who think negging is cute, it's reasonable to find you're very, very angry because you were told there would be Jims. (Or at the very least, one Jim.)

Maybe there are Jims! Maybe there are! And if there are, I'm so hyped to meet them, it's insane. But also, yeah fucking right. You mean to tell me that there's a man out there with impossibly floppy nineties hair who is also the king of intricately planned romantic gestures? Because right now I'm living in a world where dudes can barely set up a date that doesn't involve coming over to their apartment and watching them play video games while I try to find something in their kitchen that isn't PBR, so thinking about a real-life Jim is something I can't even do without my brain melting into a Jim-shaped puddle.

Oh, and wait, because there's more. Jim Halpert (and it should be noted, I am basing most of this on seasons one to four, as the character got a little hit-or-miss as the years went on so we DO NOT ACKNOWLEDGE THE LATER YEARS!!!!) wasn't confused about what he wanted, he didn't want to just "see where it went," and he didn't suggest he and Pam Netflix and chill. He met her and he knew and he acknowledged this and held out hope they'd end up together, even though she was dating some dickhead for a long time. WHO ARE YOU, JIM???? Oh, just someone who can pull off a gas station proposal and still make you think he's a goddamn dream? Cool.

Seriously, if your ex-boyfriend proposed to you in a gas station, you'd call your mom crying, but when Jim does it, it doesn't even matter and somehow it's even cuter because he couldn't wait any longer to do it and also because he is Jim. Jim, who is reliably calm and empathetic, no matter what happens. When Pam's veil tears at their wedding (if you haven't seen this show yet, I feel zero regrets about spoilers—it's, like, ten years old, dude), he doesn't tell her to get over it or panic, or just say "sorry" and move on. Nope, he compassionately cuts his own tie, thereby yet again doing anything and everything he can to make sure she's happy all the time, like it's his freaking job to make sure of it. Come. On.

Oh! And this is so fucking sad that it's worth noting, but he actually asked Pam out on a date for dinner like a normal human being. He didn't ask her if she wanted to chill or hang or come over to his place. He asked her if she was free to go to dinner with him for a first date that is a date for dating purposes. Man, it is sad that this is so rare.

And even when she rejects him, he doesn't get angry at her! There's no angry tirade about how she's a tease or a liar or a bitch. If anything, he freaking cries and BLAMES HIMSELF and apologizes for misreading signals. (I just sighed heavily.) When Pam is upset that Jim lifted her up at the karate studio, he starts to write her a formal apology email, but then does one better and buys her a bag of freaking SunChips and quietly puts them on her desk, expecting nothing in return, just so she knows he cares about her and would never intentionally upset her. I might cry soon.

He's totally happy to still be her best friend even if she never loves him back, which is just literally unreal, though it shouldn't be. He's not just being her close friend because he presumes one day they'll end up together or sleep together, and you know that because for the first few seasons, he had no reason to believe that would ever happen. So many guys only befriend you or stay in your life because they assume one day they'll get whatever it is they want from you, and the second you disprove that theory, they're out. Jim, on the other hand, would've probably still been Pam's friend even if she'd married dumb Roy and had his dumb kids because he loved her unconditionally. Jiiiiiiiiim.

Sigh.

In a world where guys will go out with you once and never talk to you again, but then like all your Instagram posts for the rest of your life like they never really wanted to date you and instead just wanted to capture you in glass and look at you forever like a caged fucking bird, Jim Halpert is a fucking revelation.

I wonder all the time if TV and movie characters are mirrors of the writers themselves, of the ways they wish they were romantic, or are romantic. I know all of my most upbeat, optimistic, romantic It Was Romance songs are one thousand percent my wishing for someone I hope exists but have no evidence of. So that is how I know. I also know so many people who claim to be romantics and identify as such, yet they are the laziest and least romantic people I've ever met. So maybe the people who write these characters just like the idea of it and have no intention of ever being that great to anyone, making my touchstone fictional love interests impossible fiction at best. But I hope not. Because otherwise I guarantee you that when my future person proposes, I will think about Jim Halpert, and then remember that he is a fictional character, and then for one second think, "But what if he isn't???" remember that he is, and then and only then reply, "Okay."

I actually did a quick search for people's favorite romantic couples and it was full of (almost exclusively white) people I wasn't that taken with, honestly. For me, I don't want to watch a "they hate each other but they love each other," because that's not what I want for myself. I also don't love the "Eh, we have a connection, but you're not what I want," so none of those couples made my list.

I truly wish TV shows and movies would change their ratings to things like "Rated R, for Really Good Romance," or "Rated PG, for Promising Gays." Throughout my life, TV and movie couples ruled everything around me, truly. I want my love to have a soundtrack for every single moment; I want music to swell when we first kiss, and for every kiss after. I don't want the wedding proposal to be the biggest moment of our lives; I want someone who proposes to me multiple times throughout our lives, and vow renewals—just numerous, constant ways we keep choosing each other and celebrating that we found each other, we did it against all odds.

One of the biggest frustrations I have with TV couples in particular is that most writers have no clue what to do with them once they get together because that's seen as boring. What a dangerous, depressing message to send to people: that the only exciting part of a relationship is before it even starts. The chase. That's all. I wouldn't be surprised if this assumption had a fair amount to do with how many people, in my generation in particular, view the world as a space with countless soul mates, countless options.

I loved Leslie and Ben on *Parks and Recreation* so much because it wasn't better when you were waiting for them to be together, or wondering if they would; it was better when they were together, by far. And while I haven't experienced that kind of love yet (yet!!!), I have experienced the "will they, won't they" shit enough to know that the buildup means nothing. I've burned out on the excitement I used to get from "I have a crush on you," because nowadays that seemingly means literally nothing. So all I hear when I hear it is, "I would fuck you," whether they mean that or not, because that's how it seems people view people and it's just the saddest thing. When I was younger and someone had a crush on me, it meant everything. I assumed it meant, "I am so taken with you, and I think you are so special, the most special, and I would love the chance to make you feel as special as you are, for as long as you'll let me." Followed by a series of formal courtship activities designed to win my heart and keep it safe and held forever. Not "FYI, I'd put my stuff in your stuff." Stop it, no.

Since the writers of many of these shows had no idea where to go from there in order to make "good TV" (see: relying on conflict instead of connection), they resorted to just killing one of them off (Freddie on *Skins* and Chris on *Skins*—what the fuck, *Skins*???), or removing everything that made them great and turning them into a bickering backbiting couple you'd never want to sit near at a restaurant (Jim and Pam), or having them circle each other through years of bad timing, which sucks the life out of their chemistry and makes you not even care when they get together in the end (Rafael and Jane).

The other frustration is that in TV shows and movies, your soul mate is always the most obvious choice. If you're a straight woman, it's your superhot, super-funny, super-supportive, clearly into you friend whom you "just don't see that way" and about whom you will (super unbelievably) say to your friends, "Really? Charles? My friend who is stupidly hot, ripped, more attractive than most people in most towns anywhere on earth, who is also super thoughtful and we have great banter and he's always there for me and he believes in me and the chemistry between us is undeniable and insanely obvious and he's kind to all my friends and gives me thoughtful gifts all the time? THAT loser? Man, I'd never even thought about dating him!"

Am I the only one who has literally thought about dating every single person I've ever met who was in my age and sexual-preference range? Even if only for a second? I've lived my whole life with every person I meet, every person I spark with, wondering if the next frame is us falling in love. So much so that I've never been able to date multiple people at once. I've never been on a first date with someone while also dating around and seeing what was up. I've treated every person I've ever been excited about (which excludes random dating-app people because I've been excited about maybe one of those ever) like this was a possible beginning of our lives together, focused on the task at hand.

In the years after Everett and I split and dating apps became more and more pervasive, I wondered if I was the only one who was still doing this whole "picking one person who seems the most special and makes you feel everything and going for it and seeing what happens" thing. And that's why I love TV and movie couples. The palpable, viscerally felt inevitability. The "even if it takes my whole life, I will win your heart" of it all. None of these men were like, "Well, I asked her to come chill on my futon and she said no, so fuck her." No. They spent years with a passive, eternal devotion to the person they loved—who, it should be noted, expressed mutual interest because I also hate this "yeah, he pursued her for years, even though she wasn't interested, until he finally wore her down" trope too—with the quiet knowledge that one day they would have everything, and no matter how long it took, no matter the number of grand gestures executed perfectly, time and again, no matter if she wasn't ready or was afraid he'd hurt her or was mentally or physically sick or had been badly hurt before, he was her person, and he was happy to show her with every word he spoke and every action he took, and he would love her always, when she was ready.

In real life, that inevitability is hilariously elusive. On any given day as a single person, you're mostly, like, "Okay, who are the people I already know are in my cast whom I spark with. I have Will, Mike, and Justin. Will has gross emotional limitations. Mike and I just talk on the internet, but it seems supersweet and I really like him. Justin is okay, but I think he's still into someone else, so he's not even remotely an option, as I require my romantic prospects to have a laser-like focus and want only me and nothing but me and see me as the only romantic option until they inevitably die. Fuck. Back to square one. I hope we're casting again soon. This show is going into season twenty-six and society tells me I need to meet my soul mate by season thirty or I'll die."

I absolutely see my life as a movie/TV show and always have. One time I told my old roommate Claire, "Aww, we're entering season two of our apartment!" because I view life like that absolutely. I'll even think, "Ooo, what if my soul mate was on like season fifteen and he's gonna come back this season because he really was a fan favorite and we've had a ratings dip because we haven't had a viable romantic option for the lead character, who is me, in literally years and the audience is getting frustrated."

Anyway, my point is I have lots of friends and leave my house with a regularity that is congruent with social norms.

HAPPY HOLIDAYS TO EVERYONE BUT YOU, YOU LONELY WEIRDO

It's hard to know when to give up the fight.
Some things you want will just never be right.

—PATTY GRIFFIN, "RAIN"

You know those dumb softball questions everyone asks you when you first meet them in an effort to have a passing knowledge of who you are as a person so they can go, "Oh, nice," and you can say, "Yeah," because we're still doing this shit for some reason? These questions are meant to be super easy, no pressure, slide into home base while walking with the casual pace of a tourist in Times Square. But for me, I'd rather you just asked me a more direct punch-to-the-face personal question.

And unfortunately for me, every year around November, these questions reach a fever pitch worthy of severe fluids and bed rest and possibly a quarantine. This is the season of "What are you doing for the holidays?" with the implied answer of "something heartwarming that makes sense to the person who asked the question. Because anything less is just too dark to even touch and you'll bum everyone out. Just keep it light or lie altogether." And I'd rather not do either option, but what else is there?

Glad you asked, me! What else is "orphan Thanksgiving" and "orphan Christmas" Facebook invites. If you're not familiar with this embodiment of an eye roll, every year around the holidays— Thanksgiving in particular—my Facebook lights up like a tacky Thanksgiving tree with the words *orphan Thanksgiving* in a bizarre number of posts, status updates, and events. For example, "OMG we're having an orphan Thanksgiving at my place for everyone who couldn't make it home for the holidays!!!" While I want to first state that I totally get that *orphan Thanksgiving* is meant to mean "We're not with our loving, wonderful families, so I guess we can be together," I would also love it if everyone could kindly stop calling it orphan Thanksgiving if the people in attendance still have a family. Especially if those families are loving as fuck.

If you have a caring, safe, living family during the holidays, I am happy to report that you have won the damn lottery and you should embrace this if you haven't already. People who have this make me super happy on some level, because it seems so rare to me and it's truly beautiful to behold, even if it also sends me reeling with personal grief that I'll never have that, I just won't, and man, wouldn't that be cool, even for a weekend.

In my experience, the people who use the term *orphan Thanksgiving* or even *orphan Christmas* seem to be blissfully unaware that it's even possible to have abusive relatives, or to have lost your parents, or to have been abandoned by your parents, or to have been kicked out of your home by your parents, or to have had to make the difficult choice to run away from or stop speaking to your family because they were unsafe, which, yes, is a thing. I know, I wish it weren't too. So who here likes drinking, am I right? (And other seamless transitions I'll attempt to make when I feel like I've gotten way too real for Gina from HR.)

To those people who live in that enviable bubble, the holidays just mean presents and twinkle lights and love and support and connection while also eating so much food. What's not to love about that? To those people, I totally get why it bums you out that you couldn't fly home for the holidays, either because you couldn't get the time off from work or because you couldn't afford the ticket. I know both of those possibilities are probably devastating to someone with a wonderful family they can't be with on the holidays, and I can't even imagine (seriously, not even a little) how much that must suck. That said, pricey flights do not an orphan make.

The word *orphan* most commonly means "someone who has lost one or both of their parents," which is typically thought to occur only when someone dies. I'm assuming the limited definition is due primarily to the fact that when the word was created, it wasn't considered socially acceptable (or at least common) to part ways with your family for any other reason. It just wasn't done, or if it was, it wasn't talked about enough to have its own nomenclature. However, I've been using that term to describe myself since I was a little kid, and later on would make these jokes about being a tree spawn as my way of being, like, "Things are not okay at home, but it's okay because I made it a joke!!!!!!! Seriously though, intervene at any time, guys, LOL. I'M NOT OKAY!"

As someone who has spent nearly every Thanksgiving by myself since I can remember, it just seems bizarre to me to use that term to describe "the thing that's not what you'd ideally be doing but is also super fun and no one is crying!" To define your experience as "gathering with your group of friends who all have totally wonderful, supportive, loving people they usually get to see on the holiday every single year, and this particular year they can't do that so that makes them orphans" sounds fucking tacky and breaks my goddamn heart.

When I attended my first "orphan" holiday gathering, it took everything I had to even leave the house to try. The party was thrown by this wonderful human I barely knew at the time and have a much greater fondness for now, Sadie, and I figured it would be great because she was great and hey, it's New York City! I'm sure if someone here is throwing an orphan holiday party, it's full of people just like me! This city is big enough and broken enough for that to be possible! It is! I paced the room, speaking to Sadie for the Appropriate Amount of Time to Speak to the Person Hosting Even Though They're the Only One You Know at the Party and You Would Literally Attach to Their Skin Like a Garfield Suction Cup on a Car Window If You Could. During this process, I found out Sadie is Jewish, so she doesn't care about Christmas: doesn't love it, doesn't hate it, it's just there. (Hello, new life goal.) The rest of the attendees, whether they knew it or not, all operated under the idea that none of us wanted to be here, we all wanted to be With Our Families, the ones we all have and love so much, am I right, guys? And I kept merging into new groups of people hoping one of them would give me a wink and a nod that said, "Psst, we're sad over here, come hang." No one did. I left early and went home and cried. There wasn't anyone like me in the world, just like I thought. Cool. Love it.

After that, if I attended any similar functions (although I no longer do, because fuuuuck that), I always attended with a heavy heart, knowing that I was being welcomed by people who probably weren't about to burst into tears at any moment. It just wasn't a heavy holiday for them as it was for me. Similar to that first night, I'd end up spending most of the night answering why I "wasn't home this year." And like before, I'd foolishly assume at least like fifty to seventy-five percent of people there shared my story, but then I'd quickly realize that nope, it was just a lot of people explaining to me, "Yeah, flights are just so expensive on Thanksgiving, I figured I'll chill here and fly home for Christmas." And then I'd try to figure out how I could excuse myself as soon as possible from the party, so I could cry in the street and remind myself this is why I isolate myself as much as possible around the holidays.

Sure, I guess I could've stayed at the party and relayed the truth. "Well, I never go home for the holidays. Also, what is a home? Is that actually a thing? Oh, it is? And everyone else has one but me? Great. Is this onion dip?" But since that response is going to heavily bum people out, I guess I'll just say, "Yep, me too," and then leave immediately because "something came up" (even if that something was, "I'm gonna go cry for six hours while I think about how I'm not like everyone else").

Look, if you still need a snappy name for your friends-gathered-at-a-holiday party, Friendsgiving is a thing, and you can call it that. You know, if you wanted to spare people who have already had hilariously painful home lives any further pain. Up to you.

Plus, it sounds way cuter and less like you're the underage cast of *Annie* gathering by a fireplace and warming your hands, wishing you could eat turkey and stuffing like children with families (though TBH both of those are gross IMO, and cranberry sauce is the only Thanksgiving food worthy of coveting, even if it looks like something Nickelodeon invented, but that's not the point).

I don't think people who use the term *orphan* mean anything malicious. I truly don't. It just goes back to that unacknowledged privilege that comes with having a loving, supportive family who makes you feel safe. It's so hard to tell people, "Yeah, the holidays kind of bum me out because my best friend as a kid was a caterpillar I kept in a muffin-tin liner in my room." You end up feeling like you don't have a place in the world because your genuine, deeply felt, and often beyond-painful feelings about your nontraditional family situation get swept under the rug in favor of easier, more "normal" frustrations with otherwise good families. And it's even worse because you're already in pain anyway, the pain of knowing you're other, and so to have to publicly hide that just reinforces what you already knew: You don't fit anywhere and you're bumming everyone out.

If you're reading this and you're, like, "BUT I LOVE CHRISTMAS!!!!" know that I am so happy for you and genuinely aspire to be you one day, instead of a caricature of Ally Sheedy in *The Breakfast Club*, hiding behind a backpack and glaring at you and your frankly very lovely decorations while I funnel Pixy Stix into my mouth.

The holidays also start so much fucking earlier when you don't have a typical family. Around the time that we get the freaking GIFT that is Halloween (aka my favorite and insanely beloved "why can't it be year-round?!" holiday, because you don't have to have anyone on earth who loves you to celebrate it, you just need to love pumpkins and goth stuff, all of which describes me), the entire world starts talking about nothing but the freaking holidays.

Commercials, movies, special TV episodes, reruns of special TV episodes, social media, advertisements, incessant emails from my bank reminding me to buy a card for people who, um, aren't great. All of it. Because everyone has a family on the holidays! The holidays are a time to spend with your family! And since everyone (EVERYONE!!!!!!!!!!!) has a perfect family they spend regular time with, everyone loves the holidays! And if you don't love the holidays, you must be a coldhearted psychopath who hates America!!! And it is just this *I Love Lucy* chocolate-factory assembly line of reminders that I don't fit, and I don't have enough pockets for all these feelings.

I spent most of my childhood doing what I've heard a lot of kids from abusive or neglectful homes do: thinking this is secretly what everyone else had too and that we were all just trying to make it to eighteen in one technically alive piece. And most of my life I've "joked" (see also: masked with humor because I'm a comedian and hence I am a pro at this) that I wish I could fall asleep on November 1 and wake up sometime around April, when all of the holidays have come and gone. (Easter depresses me too—I don't know, man, it just does.) Because hoo boy, it's a good stretch of time right there, and if you spend the holidays alone, no matter how many times you've done it, it can seem like a never-ending reminder that you don't fit (which you already knew). Every year, I swear to God, I see it coming up and I think, "Lane, you got this. It's just a day. It's just a day like any other day where you'll wake up and you'll do what you always do and you'll be fine."

I did that this year too, essentially berating myself for being a fucking baby who can't get through a few simple days. Buck up, shithead. This isn't new. But it is new. Every year the holidays roll around, I think, no matter who you are, it's brand-fucking-new to you. You bring with you whatever happened that year. If that was the year your brother died, or the year your mom told you she was ashamed of you, or the year you finally realized your dad was abusive, that's new information—or rather it's old information, but it's finally registering. So, really, there's no way of putting the holidays in their place and categorizing them as being "like all the others."

If every day we're alive, we're a ton of molecules, constantly changing and progressing, facial features and bodily organs slowly morphing as time passes, then it's literally never the same. So now, the day after Christmas, which is when I'm writing this, because why not write it when that pain is fresh as hell, I'm realizing, "Oh, I don't think I'm a weak piece of shit for not being able to handle the holidays, after a lifetime of not being able to handle the holidays." For one, I would never speak to someone that way, and two, this year was insaaaaane! I had a ton of loss and betrayal (I know this word sounds so soap-opera-y but man, sometimes people straight-up do betray you like on fucking *As the World Turns* and you're like what the hell, Diana?!) and so guess what? All that shit also followed me into the holidays. Because I'm a human being.

Anyway, if I could talk to myself and make myself hear it or wait, wait! I've got it: If a super-maternal figure could tell me the following things while brushing my hair, this would be so healing. Okay, let's do this.

Hi me,

First of all, I love you! How great are you? So great! Anyway, there are some things I want you to know if and when you're fighting through that long, cold stretch of time that seems to last as long as literally any airplane ride with a screaming baby on it:

1. No, you don't deserve this.

You're not alone during the holidays because you deserve to be— everyone deserves a great family who loves them and makes them feel safe. The fact that you never had that is not the result of your being unlovable or because something is wrong with you. I know (because I am you) that you're, like, "Duh, I know that," but seriously, around this time of year it's so easy to subconsciously think otherwise. But I know you deserve every bit as much love and normalcy as everyone else. Never doubt this. Though I know you do. Again, because I am literally you.

2. No, you're not a monster because you hate this time of year.

I hate, more than I can tell you, how much our world neglects people who have a hard time around the holidays. Do you remember [insert devastating family traumas]? Yeah, so, uh, of course you might not want to deck the halls (also you live in New York City, so you have like one hall and it's covered in weird black marks from ghosts, or rats with markers) or hear even the opening bars of "All I Want for Christmas Is You" while paying for your groceries (a true torment, though the song is pretty, yeah, yeah, I know). That's normal, and it's not because you're joyless and cold, but because you're in pain. It makes sense you'd want to avoid things that cause you more pain—that's just coping.

3. Yes, you're allowed to celebrate or not celebrate the holidays however you want.

So if you're currently prepping for the holidays via a combination of "not acknowledging the holidays at all," "turning my phone off and watching movies while eating snacks," with a possible side dish of "crying, so much crying," I support that manner of "choose your own adventure, but whatever you choose, just stay alive." Oh, also, you have every right to be spending the holidays alone or with people, crying or not crying. It doesn't make you weak or a bummer or antisocial. Most people will not understand how you have chosen to survive—and they don't need to. Fuck anyone who tells you your plans are "sad" or pressures you to be around them even though they don't feel safe or fun or you just feel like a misfit toy in the corner with one eye missing. You understand your choices and they're helping you get through it and that's enough.

4. You are marvelously strong.

I want to acknowledge all of the people reading this who have been brave enough to see their parents as harmful, because it is not an easy task. We are raised with maxims like "Blood is thicker than water" and "Respect your elders" in a culture where family, no matter how harmful, truly is everything. From an early age, a deification process begins with our parents, and even if they are flawed or harmful, they are the sun and the moon and can often remain that way. It takes, in no uncertain terms, bravery to admit to yourself, but especially out loud to other people, that your family is not safe, did not do enough, and are not people you want in your life. It flies in the face of everything our culture tells us.

In many ways, we tell people that our family members are allowed to do anything they want to us because we are theirs and they are ours forever. Self-help books often tell us "they did the *best they could," and to forgive them and let it go. That if you're still hurt or if you dare to speak the truth of what happened, you're blaming someone else for your problems. Be an adult, move on, grow up. It is not true.*

I read a book called Toxic Parents *while writing this, and some of the lines that stood out to me were these: "Children have basic inalienable rights. . . . [Their parents] must provide for their children's physical needs . . . protect their children from physical harm . . . emotional harm . . . provide for their children's needs, for love, attention, and affection." Holy shit. Really? Because most people I know didn't get that and I truly didn't know parents were required to do that. So I wanted to include it in case you, like me, sometimes think, "Well, they put a roof over my head and fed me; it wasn't their job to love me or show me affection," or, worse still, "Well, they let me live at all. It's silly I expected food and love and protection from physical and emotional harm. They were doing the best they could."*

It is so important to know we can hold our relatives, especially our parents, accountable. That regardless of "the best they could do," if you were not fed or protected or held or shown affection and love and attention, if you did not feel safe, then their best was not good enough. It just wasn't. And you are then free to do what you want with that information. Maybe that means you don't talk to them anymore, or you talk to them like you would a coworker who used to steal your lunch from the fridge—with distance and hesitance, but you are allowed to choose your own safety and well-being over the comfort level of someone who did not properly parent you.

5. Yes, it's totally normal if you get depressed even before the holidays start.

I usually get depressed like four days before pretty much every holiday (except Halloweeeeeeeeen!!!) and I always feel like, "WTF? Why am I sad?!" and then I quickly realize, "Ohhh. This holiday is coming up and that is a hard day for me and my body knows and is trying to prepare. Thanks, body, I guess."

More than anything, though, I want you to know I care about you because I know you. Not despite the fact that I know you, but because I know you. Like, I know that you sometimes lie to people and tell them you have huge plans, when your plans are to try to not get overwhelmed with the burden of your sadness in the reflection of everyone else's socially normal happiness. And I forgive you for that lie because I know why you told it—so forgive yourself for it too.

Finally, you know when people say, "Take care," and you're, like, "What the fuck do you even mean?" Well, take care. Take care of the part of you that wishes you had a "normal" family so badly it kills you. Take care of the part of you that will never understand why your family was the way they were, or is the way they are, or is no longer around at all. Take care of the part of you that feels "other" throughout the holiday season. And more than anything, feel proud of yourself, because you didn't let being other kill you. You're still here, and one day maybe you'll have a family of your own and you'll love the holidays. Or maybe you'll never like this time of year. Either way, you'll still be here, living. Sometimes that's the bravest thing of all. And if you don't believe me, it's a line in Buffy the Vampire Slayer, *and as I and I both know, that show is everything.*

———

If you're spending the holidays alone, for whatever reason, and you need tips, I can tell you what I do for the holidays and you can pick and choose which ones sound smart and cool and which ones sound deeply sad.

First thing you need to know is the hours of every single grocery store you might need to go to, just in case. In my experience, most places just close early on Thanksgiving, so you usually have until, like, five p.m. to get what you need, but go at like ten a.m. It's usually not that crowded then and just gets crowded later in the day when people realize, "Oh, shit, I forgot to buy free-range butter. Also, what is free-range butter? Man, my aunt Christine is a LOT." At Christmas, stores usually close early on Christmas Eve and stay closed all day on Christmas, so, bitch, you need to stock up. And some stores will also be closed the day after Christmas too, so just yeah, buy more than you think you need. Especially because if you're sad, you should absolutely not also be hungry.

In most of the years I've lived in New York City, I've spent the holidays several different ways. For many of them, this included going to the children's playground near my house and swinging on the swings alone and singing along to my headphones super loud, which I love. That said, in the last year I've started pointing out that park to my friends when we walk by it and saying, "Look!!! That's where I used to spend Christmas and Thanksgiving every year! Oh, shit, that's unbearably sad. I hear it now." It just never occurred to me. To me, I was doing something I loved in a place that was all my own. But it is real sad.

Now I just use the holidays as an opportunity to do whatever the hell I want. Sleep, watch movies, not move, skip the gym, go to the gym, eat literally whatever I want, damn the cost, sky's the limit, you earned it, this day is tough. It becomes a massive treat-yourself day for me, and I'm sure in the future I'll work in massage or a treatment in which I get covered in gemstones by kittens or something.

I also greatly recommend staying the hell off social media. You'll tell yourself it's no big deal, it's fine, but the winter holidays, along with Mother's Day and Father's Day, are hell for people without traditional families. It's just a sea of people posting about how much they love their families and photos of them doing normal family things. It's totally possible their families are as complex and painful as yours, but this will not occur to you while you're sifting through photos of them playing Monopoly with a bunch of elderly people you'll never meet.

And if you never had proper parents, or they weren't great to you, even if you see posts about someone saying they miss so-and-so relative who died last year, it's so easy to go to that place of, "COOL, WELL, I NEVER EVEN GOT AN AWESOME DAD, AT LEAST YOU GOT ONE," an anger you don't mean at someone you probably love, but this day is just too much of a powder keg of emotions for you to have that kind of distance from your emotions.

In the end, Thanksgiving is one day and Christmas is like 1.5. My whole life it felt like years getting through those days, but once I realized, "Hey, darlin', we just have to get through this one day and then done, back to normal. It's just one day in your life, so let's really enjoy it. Now what do we want to do?" I realized it's so get-through-able.

So put your phone away (unless talking to someone makes you

feel better), because social media is not your friend right now (ugh, even one tweet about "remember your family is everything" or "call your grandparents, guys," can seem lethal) and do something you truly love. If you wanna play music all day and dance, do it! If you wanna go to a dog park and watch dogs, do it! If you wanna watch a movie or TV show that doesn't have strong familial themes in it (because that's a whole other thing), do it! If you wanna be unprecedentedly lazy when you'd normally lose your shit over that kind of decadence, now's the time.

Just be even gentler with yourself than you'd think you'd need to be. You already survived everything you survived, so give yourself a day where you allow yourself to stay present (or numb off entirely) in this one day of your life. You can truly make this day whatever you want it to be. If nothing else, do it as a gift to yourself—someone who deserves it more than you will ever know.

ALL THIS PAIN MUST BE WORTH IT BECAUSE YOU'RE SUPPOSED TO BE MY SOUL MATE

You were a wolf in the daylight
And you almost had me.

—LIGHTS, "ALMOST HAD ME"

After realizing that most of the people I was choosing to date as an adult were genuine nightmares, I decided to do all the dumb things we tell women to do to find love. Sure, men's instructions for finding a girlfriend are usually "Be Born, Wake Up, Brush Your Teeth (Optional)—and boom, you get girlfriend! Now relax and enjoy girlfriend!"

But with women, we tell them to do all the things I decided to do. I would take time off from dating, I would let love find me, I would meet someone through my friends, I would stop looking and focus only on myself, and if I met anyone great, we would be friends first, yeah! I would go to (more) therapy, I would work out, I would go through all of the hoops to be ready enough to "deserve" the love I wanted. What could go wrong?

And what could go wrong was Max. Max was someone I'd known through mutual friends (score!), we were friends first (score!), I hadn't dated anyone seriously in years (score!), I was focused on my career and working on myself so I could be the partner I wanted (score score score!).

When Max and I reconnected, she told me everything I'd ever wanted someone to say to me—and also happened to be a codependent love addict who had just gotten out of a relationship like two hours prior.

When we reconnected, Max hadn't worked as a hair stylist in several years. She was taking odd jobs and fixing cars, and as is my way, I knew I had a mission to help her become everything she must be (ugh). I hate that in so many ways, on a deeper level, so many women are still set up to think like housewives from the 1950s, helping our husband negotiate a raise while stuffing down our own ambitions, because this sucks and I want my money back. And by money back, I mean I want all the hours, money, and time spent making men and masculine-presenting women's careers better and putting their needs before my own, because, oh man, it does not pay to be that kind of Good Girl.

As I'm looking back at the text chain, it's full of her telling me all my exes and suitors didn't "appreciate or give you nearly enough. Not even close." We discussed our favorite power couples and, in true queer-lady form, our astrological planets and rising signs and shit. Who knew her chart was actually best translated as "Run, Lane"?

She told me the first time she met me she knew we were soul mates. But since she had a girlfriend at the time (and literally always), she knew she should stay away from me so she wouldn't have to face that she was in love with me.

She came on strong and then some. She quickly established herself as my primary confidante and emotional support system, making me feel safe and being there for me when I really needed someone.

To the point where I, like so many times before, wished she didn't text me every three seconds from sunup to sundown and send me so many videos, because it felt like her whole life revolved around me, and in her mind, we were already married, a dynamic that has marred my relationships before—Adam from high school all over again.

She told me that she knew she had work to do on herself but asked me to give her a year. She clarified that she didn't want to make me wait for her and I could date whomever I wanted in the meantime, but if at the end of that year I was still single, I was the person she wanted to be with. (Is this sounding like some Everett shit? Because I'm seeing now it was!)

She told me elaborate things she'd done for past partners that now read like false advertising—highway billboards promising the best, most well-photographed steak you've ever had in your life, but then you pull over and it's week-old, off-brand Hamburger Helper.

She told me that if she was ever to propose to me, she'd do it all the time, every few years, to keep me on my toes, just to remind me how many times over she would marry me. She seemed like everything I'd ever wanted. And before I knew it, I believed in her like religion.

She'd Seamless me food when I hadn't eaten all day, she'd send groceries to my hotel room on tour, with my favorite flowers and my favorite chocolate bar, or my favorite drinks. She took care of me in the same ways Everett had, but she also seemed to truly support me, truly see me. She loved everything I was, which was so much more than "a pretty girl who—uh, what do you do again?" She loved that I shone so brightly and was so ambitious. And she wanted to be there in the race with me, handing me Gatorade and kissing my forehead before I went back out there.

I wanted to believe her so badly, but it was hard to because of past experiences. At some point I said, as I often do—a plea to the person on the receiving end—"I'm trying so hard to believe you, I really am. I'm trying so hard to let people in and I'm just afraid." And I would, if I could, go back in time and tell myself that I had every right to be afraid of her, to believe the warning bells.

I wasn't having dumb LOL trust issues because of my dumb LOL entire life full of people who gave me every good—nay, great—reason to have trust issues; I was having issues with trusting someone who should never be trusted, and that issue was trying to protect me . . . but all I could do was berate it for speaking up on my behalf. And it was such a pity.

She'd sign her texts, "Thinking of you always," and I'd gently remind her we weren't going to do that, remember? And that I didn't want a long-distance relationship, and she needed to heal herself. I was trying to talk someone out of patterns that ran so deeply she couldn't even see she was repeating them. She agreed, she needed time to heal her codependency, "You're right, you're right."

Days later, I got a package full of presents for my tour: bath bombs, flowers, toothpaste, a little bento box, other cute little things. And a letter signed, "Yours, always." I got so angry I threw the bento box down and cried. The person who kept telling me to set boundaries kept violating mine, saying she wanted to be my girlfriend, but not yet, and then saying she was ready, but me telling her to slow down, and her saying she would, and then all of a sudden, she was "mine, always," whether I wanted that or not.

Then one night, something shifted. She didn't get a job she wanted and she withdrew a frightening amount and went so dark I couldn't see her, couldn't reach her. To save her (see also: to get her to not abandon me), I took a break from my "I haven't eaten or slept or stopped working in fifteen hours" day to make her a playlist to soothe her, wrote her a long email reminding her how incredible she was, started working on a short film so she could work on set with me, sent her voice memos letting her know I was there, and bought a shirt to give her when she came to visit. I poured it all out. Every bit I had. And she took them all and closed the door behind her. And this is why anxious attachment people shouldn't date fucking avoidant people.

I then became the one who refused to see the red flags, and would go on to rip myself inside out every weekend for a month, explaining myself over and over again, like the right words would bring the other Max back. I should've just skipped the metaphors and run, because you can't untie those knots when you're not even the one who tied them. People have these entire worlds, entire histories inside of them, with thousands of knots tied by people you'll probably never meet and will never know, so your helping to untie them is just not a thing. And I would know, because I would've gladly walked through fire a thousand times if it would've erased the hurt she'd experienced, untied all the knots that kept her locked in a cycle of abuse and shutting down.

I'd met a guy that previous fall, just before Max came back into my life. He was a human rights lawyer named Chris who was visiting from Australia. He'd come to Tinder Live with his brother and came up to me afterward to tell me how much he'd loved it, but I had a terrible flu that night and was barely able to stand. He asked me to add him on Facebook, offering to help me bring Tinder Live to Australia, and I pushed the buttons with my fevered hands, but Facebook didn't work, so he asked for my number and I gave it, thinking nothing of it, and went home to pass out. But he texted me throughout the entire time I was sick and was so sweet and couldn't stop telling me how funny I was and how much he loved the show, and checking in on me. And when I got better, he asked if I wanted to hang out before he left.

I showed up to the bar absolutely not thinking it was a date and wore glasses and a hoodie. About two minutes in, he used the word *date* and I said, "Wait, what?" and he laughed and said, "Yeah, I think you're amazing." And I thought, "Hmm, okay, why not?" We walked around my neighborhood for hours and he was so charming and sweet and we kept stopping so he could buy us drinks to stay hydrated through our epically long walk-and-talk date. Once we got to my house, we kissed and it was good. I thought about inviting him up and then remembered I'm me and not a TV character and told him to have a good night.

The next morning he texted me saying he knew how much I love Halloween and he and his friends were going to rent a car and drive to Long Island to see this 10,000 carved pumpkins thing that sounded so dope and he would love it if I came with him. I was thrilled because that sounded like the best first date ever. He picked me up and it was THE BEST NIGHT EVER BECAUSE HALLOWEEN and I kept wanting to hold his hand, and sometimes we would, but I kept reminding myself, "Lane, he doesn't live here! He's just some dude on holiday from Australia! Please calm down." And I did. After we got back home, I knew he was leaving town again the next morning, so I figured my usual plan of waiting "several months before we decide if we are emotionally ready to take this to the next level" before sleeping with him wouldn't work. So he came upstairs and we fooled around. And it was so, so bad. Just, bad bad bad bad bad. But the next day I left for tour, and he left for his next vacation destination.

But we kept talking, even though I had a bitter taste in my mouth from the shitty hookup. One night after an out-of-town gig, the company I was working for shorted me money I'd been killing myself to make and I just broke, cried-so-much-I-lost-my-voice broke. I texted him and said I knew it was like three a.m. there and he didn't know me well, but this had happened and I was a mess. He said, "Call me if you want! I'm up." And so I did. And he talked to me until six a.m. about it and really listened, so sweetly, and was so comforting and affirming and kind. So the next day I told him, "Hey, can I tell you something? That hookup was bad. And look, I know you're some Australian lawyer dude who was in town for a week and you just wanted to hook up with me, but it was not cool." And I listed all the reasons why it wasn't great and he eagerly listened and agreed and apologized, but then added, "I didn't just want to sleep with some-one. I really like you, I think you're amazing. If we lived in the same city, I'd absolutely date you, but I'm just glad I get to know you now and I'd love to see you when we both get back to New York before I fly back to Australia, if you want." And I really did want.

We spent his last day in town together watching movies and hooking up again (better this time) and falling asleep together, with his brother texting him before he went to bed, "Aww, are you stay-ing at Lane's?" because he'd been at my Tinder Live show too, and he'd told his brother how much he liked me and it was the sweetest thing. Before he left, he took me to breakfast and we kissed goodbye and that was that. But we still talked here and there before he asked me, that same spring I was "with" Max, to come with him on an all-expense-paid trip to Iceland, where I'd always wanted to go. I told Max he'd asked me and she told me she was actually going to ask me the same thing that night. And she was hurt that I would even consider going with him, but added that I was allowed to go because she couldn't be with me yet, but also she was hurt, so . . . (eye roll).

So somehow in one night, I was asked by two people to go to Iceland, what the fuck? Anyway, I thought about it for weeks, how much I wanted to go with him because it would be light and fun, and if I went with Max, then our first date would be a trip to a foreign country and that was the opposite of taking it slow. Plus, I knew we'd get even closer and it'd kill me to come back home alone, without her, after being with her that much, finally, in Iceland. More than anything, I decided I couldn't go with Chris. It wasn't right. Sure, things weren't great with Max and me right then, but she was going to marry me and she was my person and this was just a rough patch. I wanted to do the sweet, rom-com movie moment thing of telling her I was choosing her, that I would always choose her.

When I told her I was choosing her, she yelled at me and told me I should've gone with Chris, because we weren't anything and I should go. I told her I didn't want to, I wanted her, and she got very quiet again.

I will never understand how, just as quickly and intensely as she entered, she could and would exit my life as though she'd never said a word to me. Never felt anything for me or because of me. And I'd just become a girl she knew once, kind of, from a distance.

If you beg people, "Please, I've already been through enough. Take good care of my heart because I won't be able to handle it if you don't," and they say, "Of course, darling," and then proceed to break everything in your life anyway, because fuck you, what do you do with that? Max and I got to the point where I'd internalized the dynamic of her setting the boundaries, ignoring mine, and taking all she needed, despite my asking her not to. And I stopped eating. It took me weeks to realize I was trying not to need anything so I could be perfect for her, so she could take and I'd never need anything back. Like she seemingly wanted.

Chris is still someone I talk to now and then. He'll text me to let me know he's thinking of me, or that he told an American he met in Australia about my Tinder Live shows and told him he should go. He tells me how proud he is of me, that I'm gorgeous and funny and special. Looking back, Chris was the secure attachment I could've chosen, but I chose Max. Not because I consciously knew she wasn't a secure attachment, but because deep down, my brain wanted to go down that road because this is the road I know.

I didn't understand how someone who seemed to be everything I'd wanted in a person could also become someone so harmful. I had vetted her. I had done everything right. I had worked on myself. Years had passed and I was so much wiser than I was before.

And yet again I was in a situation like I was with Everett. Someone who claimed to be everything I wanted, but I could feel that they weren't, all the time. But then I told myself, as I had before, that maybe no one's perfect and no one gets everything they want in a partner, a concept that has remained eternally depressing to me on all levels ever since it was introduced. And if that's actually true, and everyone's just totally okay with it, why isn't that in people's wedding vows? "Well, Sharon is basically everything I want, like, mostly. Like, okay, for sure I thought this would be more fun or more romantic, or feel more like some kind of destiny or fate, like coming home to somewhere I've never been before and yet feels more familiar to me than anything in my entire life ever has. But fuck it, Sharon loves the Dodgers, and I do too, so let's rock this!"

The idea of Greg (that guy's name is Greg, it just is) making that choice to bloom where he's planted because, whatever, man, he's not getting any younger and Sharon's an all right chick, is depressing as shit. But on the other hand, Greg probably isn't sitting in his room with his laptop right now imagining a place that must exist, it just has to, though there's little evidence to support it. No, Greg is probably

happily sharing a Frito pie microwaved in an upside-down Dodgers commemorative plastic hat with Sharon, the woman he wants
to share all future Frito pies with for the rest of their lives, maybe,
probably, we'll see, who knows.

But I am not a Greg.

Max finally came into town to visit me so we could put an end to
this *You've Got Mail* shit. During the time she was here, we played a
couple for that whole month, with her taking as many breaks as she
felt like to let me know I meant nothing to her.

I went to hang out with her friends at a bar and heard her joke
about how single she was while I seethed. The following day she joked
that I'd probably flirted with someone at that bar and that, for the
record, I totally could've hooked up with anyone there. Confused and
annoyed, I looked at her and said, "Why would I do that? I literally
came to that bar to meet your friends and only hung out with them all
night because I'm crazy about YOU." And she launched into more of
her bi-phobic bullshit about how "I know this is bi-phobic, but I don't
trust bisexuals." What a cool tune. Seriously, this shit is so much worse
coming from lesbians and gay people than it is from straight people.
Get your shit together, assholes.

Those people (and shitty TV shows who make cheap jokes about
bisexuality not being a thing) have no idea how much time bisexual
and queer people spend thinking about their sexuality. The world
desperately wants anyone who isn't simply straight, or simply gay, to
pick a side and stick to it. Personally, no one has ever told me to pick
a label, but I can feel it in my gut that I need to, and oftentimes I see
it reflected in other people. If I have a friend who knows me to date
only one gender and I start dating someone of a different gender, I
find myself playing the pronoun-dodging game. I start saying things
like "*This person* I have a crush on" and how "*they* are really great,"

just so I can avoid people asking me to categorize it, when all I want to do is be psyched because I like someone. Or there's the good friend of mine who identifies as straight but will often say she's attracted to women but she's "not gay" and is "definitely straight." I hear her say this and want to hug her and tell her it's okay to not pick a word and to be attracted to whomever she's attracted to, but I also know why she feels that's impossible.

What if you fall outside all the boxes? What are you supposed to do then, other than wrestle with the feelings of otherness, the "oh shit, my sexual-identity deadline is here and I don't have all my paper-work filled out yet"? There really is something about being able to put yourself into one concise, well-marked, tidy section of society, dusting your hands off on your pants. "That's that. Now I can move on with my day." But it's not that simple.

If you're a queer woman, you've probably spent time changing your online dating profile to read *straight* when you wanted to meet men, and *lesbian* when you wanted to meet women, because you desperately want to avoid men who think you're looking for a three-way and women who think you're slutty and not to be trusted. And let me tell you something, on any given day and in any given room, I typically want to sleep with zero people in it. I'm open to being attracted to any gender and rarely attracted to any, so miss me with this stupid idea that in any room everyone is appealing to me because they're technically a gender I have dated. Let me briefly affirm that you choose your labels. You choose those you show them to. You choose when the labels change, if they change. None of us is just one of anything. If I'm funny right now, I might be really sad in two hours. That doesn't change the fact that I'm funny; it just means that there's been a shift. I think many of us are much more sexually fluid than we think we are; we're just so scared

of what that means, and that we have to take action. And I'd just like to tell you that you don't.

I let the bi-phobic and frankly incredibly tired comment slide, and by that I mean pushed it further down into the reserve of anger and resentment and things left unsaid, needs left chronically unmet, and a constant underlying current of emotional abuse I hadn't felt this violently since my childhood.

When I first started dating Max, I felt like I'd finally broken free of my relationship blueprints. I had vowed to never again repeat what I'd done with Everett, not to continue to run at any sign of potential trouble. This time I was going to assume there wasn't a "but then" with her and that she was everything she said she was. She seemed so nurturing and communicative and self-aware and kind that I was sure I'd beat the system. "Man, these years of therapy have finally paid off! I've broken the cycle! I'm free! I'm finally dating someone healthy! Woohoooooo!!!" But just as soon as I was sure I was in the clear, it was as if she'd pulled off her mask and said, "Haha, surprise, motherfucker! I'm basically your parents. I just waited way longer to reveal that, so you felt safe!" and I was, like, "OH, COME ON!!!"

I had finally let my guard down, but with the completely wrong person.

That night, once more with feeling, I told her in full recap form everything she'd put me through. I lay in her lap while fighting for breath between crying. "I tried to do everything perfectly, to navigate every quickly shifting curve you threw at me daily, constantly changing the rules, and I tried so hard to be perfect. I tried so hard. And I loved you so much. And why, why, why are you doing this to me?"

She cried and held me and told me, "Lane, you couldn't have done it perfectly. I set up a game that was impossible for you to win and you did nothing wrong. There was no way you could've done this the right way, I changed the rules every day and I know that. I should've protected you and I didn't. I should've protected us and I didn't. I set us up to fail and I know it."

I knew this was a conversation like the thousands of others in which she would have a moment of clarity and insight and owner-ship of what she'd done, and acknowledge the colossal damage she'd caused, but in all likelihood, any recently developed insight would vanish by morning, just as it did when I had similar conversations with my family as a child. I wanted to push her away, make her leave, but I also didn't want to be alone. And I remembered that feeling well—the feeling of being held in the arms of the one who hurt you. And still thinking, "This is better than nothing."

To make it up to me, Max offered to take me to dinner, and I somehow ended up paying, as I always did. This was one of the most painful, familiar things she'd do: the "let me take care of you, just kid-ding, I'm not" move that she'd become a fucking pro at while she was here. This was coupled with her reminders that "I owe you money. I'm keeping track, don't worry! I'm really good at that," even though I rarely saw a dime.

In the morning, her cab came and she hugged me and said, "I love you," and I said, "I love you too." Exhausted by her and by this rancid version of what we could've been, I texted her while she was flying and told her maybe we should just take the pressure off this and be friends for a while. She said that would be great because then she could focus more on trying to get a job at a salon in New York so we could be together.

In the days that followed, she mostly ignored me and detached from me. I barely existed. So my friend offered me some acid and I took it, and I hadn't done that since I was a kid. (What a sentence. Seriously, if you ever hear me say, "Man, I feel like a kid again!" call 911.) I told her and she, a person who knew I was sober, thought it was funny. I thought it was a red flag that I was decimated by her and by this, but hey, six to one. A few days later, she was house-sitting for some married friends and she sent me a video saying she wanted this so badly, to be in a couple and to have a house and a dog, to be so in love with someone. This was her pattern—back and forth. Two days before, she was telling me she loved me and wanted to move here to be with me, and just days later, I was a platonic friend listening to her bitch about her love life.

I finally told her I needed a break and I gave her the space to do what people do in movies when you tell them you can't live like this anymore and they need to get help or else they'll lose you. And then, because they're so scared of losing you, they really pull it together and pull out all the stops to win you back! And you won't be surprised to know none of that happened. Instead, she told me she'd been doing great, her whole life was on track, self-esteem bordering on cocky, and no more need for me. She even added the delightful touch of saying she still loved me, but couldn't be with someone who thought she needed to change. You know, because I'd asked her to change so she could stop hurting me all the time. That was unfair of me to want.

People who reject you for being broken after they're the ones who broke you, or who act like they're not the problem and the problem is the issues you had before them, are evil. They just are. And also, it's, like, "Yeah, but you compounded those preexisting issues like interest, asshole."

Truly, to break someone that much, for that long, and to then tell them the reason you're ending it is because they asked you to stop breaking them, and if you were a better person, you'd be okay with having them break you, is soulless at best.

When you have a lot of shine to you, as so many bighearted people often do, you can attract a lot of people easily, because people are drawn to it, that kind of light. It can be so easy to forget that not everyone deserves your shine. But when you spend so much of your earliest years being told you have no shine at all, even though you're pretty sure maybe you do, and someone finally tells you they see it too, you do, you have it, you want to give them everything. Because of this, more often than not, you're not falling in love with them, you're using them as a way to fall in love with yourself.

Weeks later, I found out she'd been cheating on me for months. She once told me she was terrified she'd become just like her cheating grandparent, whom everyone always said she was most like. And all of her previous fears about that had proved shockingly true, but then again, this many lies and stress-related illnesses I'm still healing from, what was really shocking about any of this? I can't describe to you how it feels to go from thinking you have a true partner, true best friend, and true soul mate to seeing that person become your abuser—and then seeing them cheat on you and see that maybe you were a mark all along, a pawn in a game you didn't see coming that played out exactly the way they intended.

I've experienced so many shades of this before, and all I can say is this: If you see a woman who is working super hard to become who she's meant to be and to achieve the things she wants to achieve, and you have nothing to add to her life or to give back to her in any way, please just leave her the fuck alone.

HOW TO BE ALONE

A lot of people enjoy being dead. But they are not dead, really.
They're just backing away from life. *Reach* out. Take a *chance*.
Get *hurt* even. But play as well as you can. Go, team, go! Give
me an *L*. Give me an *I*. Give me a *V*. Give me an *E*.
L-I-V-E. Live! Otherwise, you got nothing
to talk about in the locker room.

—MAUDE, *HAROLD AND MAUDE*

Just after Max and I ended things, I'd found out I was going to be in
the *Out* 100, which is a list of influential LGBTQ people as listed by
Out magazine. It's huge and I was so touched, even if I was living in
my own personal queer nightmare. Man, when people say, "I wish I
could date women, it'd be so much better," I want to show them my
box of evidence to the contrary. The shoot ended up happening just
two days after I found out about the cheating. I cried the whole way
there and told the photographers and makeup artists I'd just had a
"bad breakup," which obviously doesn't begin to cover it.

The incredibly sweet and warm photographers and stylists showed
me Mariah Carey's apartment, which was across from where we were

shooting (I did not scream "OMG, I used to practice hitting high notes to your songs while sliding down the stairs!!!" at her window and I really regret that now), and reminded me I was beautiful, something that had been beaten out of me in that relationship more times than I'd realized. My favorite part of the shoot was when the art director looked at the shots they were getting and said, "You said you were just getting out of a bad relationship, right?" and I said, "Yeah," and he said, "Oh, we're gonna find you someone so much better." And I lit up at the very idea. Of someone seeing my face in these photos and thinking, "What a special, beautiful person. I should be so lucky to date her," a sentiment I hadn't heard or felt in what seemed like years.

And again, in that instant, I felt held and seen. They couldn't know what those words meant to me, or what it meant to have the contrast of immense pain in my life, but also a roomful of designer clothes in my size that were just for me, and a team of people who were all there to take my photo and play around with me while I was wearing seventies roller skates I could barely stand in, because I had done the work I'd set out to do for my community. And even if I felt so completely alone right now, this was an acknowledgment that I was, in some way, not alone at all. Sure, I was coming out of some shit with a bi-phobic person who was so cruel to me I still can't absorb it, but the other people in the queer community thought I was special and important and worthy of good things.

About a week later, I booked my dream trip to Prince Edward Island, home of Anne of Green Gables. I'd had a lifelong dream to go there, live there, and fall in love there. I'd put it off for months, due to my basing my entire life on Max. What if I booked it at a time when she was here in New York? What if I booked it at a time when she was going to surprise me and come here? Later, on the plane to PEI, I laughed at this because I would've been shocked if she'd been capable of basic human emotions toward the end, let alone grand romantic gestures that weren't entirely self-serving.

It's insane the kinds of rewrites you have to do when you find out who someone really is. You have to rewire and reroute your entire brain. ("I want to text Max." [*Takes self by the shoulder and reroutes her to the other direction.*] "No, she doesn't exist. Not anymore, and she never did." "But . . ." "I know, sweet pea. I know." "I miss her so much, she's the person I love," "No, she's not. It was all a lie, Laney. You don't know that woman. You don't love her. You just love who she pretended to be, and she pretended to be that woman so that you would love her.") It's like training a dog not to shit all over your house, but instead you're training yourself not to be with someone who shit all over your life. After we broke up, I realized I might as well book the trip. And I did. Thank god.

I booked my flight pretty down to the wire, a few weeks before, but fortunately flights were still pretty reasonable, which I would later learn was attributable to the fact that I was going to PEI in the fall, just after their tourism season ended and basically on the very last possible day to go there before every business shuttered for the season, and every homeowner bolted their doors to fend off the torturous winter.

I went for eight days. I packed the small tote bag I always bring with me no matter where I go or for how long. I brought three lightweight lacy sundresses so I could go full-on American Anne Fan Woohoo. (I would very quickly regret this once I got there, since it was max fifty-nine degrees every day.) I brought my Dolly Parton hoodie given to me by Stephanie in Atlanta, four pairs of underwear, two pairs of wacky knee socks with hearts on them, one pair of sneakers, and just a ton of face masks. And I hopped on the puddle jumper plane and landed and got a car without extra insurance or roadside assistance because, wow, what a badass.

I've traveled by myself exclusively for as long as I can remember, but apparently people don't do it that often. Movies and TV and friends have made it very clear to me that people travel in packs, in groups, but I never did. I never moved anywhere where I already knew people, never moved to a neighborhood because I had friends over there, never took a Girls' Trip (???). I never even thought about it. That was what other people with families and normal lives did and I just figured there were no exceptions. That, and I wasn't sure where I'd go and also LOL poverty and survival.

When I arrived in the area of my friend Caissie's vacation home/ church (that she generously lets her friends stay in when she's not there—THANK YOU, CAISSIE!!!) in the middle of nowhere, I couldn't remember what it looked like at all. She'd sent me photos but I was still in my zombie post-breakup brain mode, so I was barely functioning. The second I saw the house and the road leading up to it, I squealed. I got inside and the church was freezing and I couldn't get the heat to work, but I didn't care. I googled the nearest grocery store and loaded up on whatever I thought I'd need for the week.

The first thing I did when I got back was throw my bag down and belt out Neko Case's "John Saw That Number," which was just meant to be belted in a church with incredible acoustics. Over the next week, I did a series of Kitchen Karaoke posts (Instagram videos of me singing in my kitchen while chopping vegetables) every single night because the church was so beautiful and my voice sounded so strong and so crisp and I could really hear myself, as if I were listening to someone else sing.

The next morning I went to the restaurant nearby that I was told had Lane-friendly foods and asked a woman I saw waiting tables, who looked like a young Mrs. Claus—just super happy and cheery, with full red cheeks that made you want to hug her—if they had things that were both vegan and gluten-free, so I wasn't resigned to my typical no-man's-land of side salads and granola bars. She looked at me and said, "Oh, yes, dear! All of our desserts today are actually vegan and gluten-free." I got so excited I said, "Oh my god, honestly, my first instinct is to hug you right now." She laughed and said, "Well, bring it in, girl!" and we hugged.

I told her I was Caissie's friend from New York City and she told me her name was Allison, and we talked as I ate poutine for the first time and she sat with me once everyone left and we chatted and she introduced me to her husband. They ran the restaurant together and lived upstairs and it was just the sweetest thing. The restaurant was equal parts delightful small-town diner and monument to all the years they'd been married—which was exactly why I'd come to PEI. To remember that I once believed in love, that I once was a romantic. That I once lived and breathed people's love stories, even though that part of me had been murdered like a *Law & Order: SVU* victim found in a river.

I told Allison it was so much colder than I'd expected and she offered to give me an extra coat and told me I could keep it the whole trip if I brought it back before I left. I brought it back the next day, partly because I found a dream sweater at a nearby thrift store, and partly because I have a weird thing about borrowing things, where I worry that I might forget to give it back and therefore I will not be perfect, so I'd rather someone just take it back before I've even used it so I don't have a chance to mess up even once!!!

I ended up spending part of every day over there, holding her granddaughter, who was an adorable little infant, and telling them I was um, kind of working on a book and that I, uh, sort of did comedy. Careful not to brag, but also, I do some kind of cool things and anyway, how's the flan?

And I explored the city. I went to Lucy Maud Montgomery's childhood home and cried the entire time, mostly about how much I identified with her my whole life, especially as I got older and realized this woman, who had inspired untold levels of romanticism in the hearts of so many through her novels, was also deeply depressed and lonely, a parallel with my own life I could not have predicted. Every room felt touched with magic. I even snuck away and stood in front of the Lake of Shining Waters and cried some more, gently singing to soothe myself and also as a celebration of how much joy I felt bursting from me, just by being that in touch with the hopeless romantic I used to be, and maybe still was. I took some flowers from the surrounding area and placed some in my hair, and later pressed them into a book. They now hang over my bed as a reminder of who I was, am, and could be again, if I could find my way back to it.

I went to Charlottetown (the urban part of PEI) and was surrounded by guys who looked exactly like the super-sweet, good-natured, super-romantic, and relationship-driven men I knew in my small town, whom I miss so much. And it felt so good to be flirted with by someone who you know full stop would've been so happy to get to take you to dinner and have even an hour of your time to make you feel special. My whole body just relaxed as I typed that—it feels that rare, healing, and refreshing.

I went to a large rec center outside the city where they had a pool and bowling and I went in to bowl. (I will always choose swimming or being in water over bowling, but I'd gone in the pool and a baby puked next to me, so I was given a bowling voucher and was, like, "Okay, sure.")

There was literally no one there, but I was gonna lean into this manic pixie dream girl moment so hard. So I punched in all the players as Lane, Also Lane, and Still Lane. All three of us played two games and spoiler: I won. And it was so ridiculous and funny and super fun. And the teen who was manning the booth and definitely watching me play with three different mes, for multiple rounds and two whole games, was either identifying me as his future dream girl or keeping his hand on the button to call the cops if he needed to. Who can say which!

I went to see the Bottle Houses, which are a series of houses made out of recycled bottles. And when I went in to buy my ticket, the clerk said, "You're driving around here all by yourself? All alone?" and I smiled and said, "Yep." And she said, "Doesn't that feel scary?" and I smiled again and said, "Nope. I'm good." Remembering all the times when I was alone before and I hadn't been good, preparing me for this moment when I was.

I walked along the beach and made friends with a woman who lived nearby and petted her dog, who she said usually doesn't like people. I love that. When a dog who doesn't really like people immediately loves me, it's the greatest compliment. That reassurance that someone can see your goodness from miles away. She told me you could eat seaweed straight out of the ocean and we did and it was the freest, most little kid feeling. Of knowing things could still be new, that there were still so many good things left to experience.

Before I headed back, Allison and I had deeper conversations about my past and this book. She held my face in her hands and told me, "You are so lovable. It's just so evident. You meet you for twenty seconds and you just know how lovable you are. And I don't say this lightly, but I'd love for you to be one of my kids. And I mean that."

I had no clue what to do with this. It was the second time it had happened and I couldn't get hurt again. She also told me about some horrifying things she'd experienced that she'd never told anyone about, not even her family, and I was so humbled that she was able to share that with me. I have always had that effect on people and it's a true honor, but also often very heavy because I hate that anyone has ever been in any pain ever. And hearing it makes it real. And feeling powerless and unable to remove it from their heart is even more real.

The night before my return flight, she told me to come by the café and she'd pack me some snacks for the flight because I "couldn't take that trip without having snacks." I looked around, like, "Uh, I could live off a sleeve of rice cakes if I needed to," again stuck in that mode of "oh I CAN" instead of the newfound world of "but you don't have to" that I was trying to acclimate to. She packed me tortilla chips and hummus and veggies and ginger snaps and I ate them up, emotionally first and physically later. While she packed the chips, I said, "And it's great because you can just give me the crumbs too, so you don't waste those!" and she replied, "Oh, I'll give you the whole chips, and we do use those crumbs in our Frito pie!" Thankfully, she didn't pick up on my vibe of "Feel free to give me the garbage!!!!! Look how easy I am to love!!!!! I'm like an unkillable succulent!! Just pay attention to me every eight months, but please take me home, any amount of care will work for me!!!"

Totally bizarrely, she'd also asked me about the rest of my Tinder Live tour dates for that month for the United States, and it just so happened I was going to be doing a show in San Antonio right when she was there. So when I got to San Antonio, she came to my show with her friend and it was the strangest and best thing. She'd grown up in San Antonio and was going back to see her mom the same weekend I was there. She took me to thrift stores with her and even showed me the house she grew up in. And I'll remind you, this was just a diner owner I'd met a few times. But of course this was happening. Of course. Every time she hugged me or told me she was worried about me or wanted to make sure I'd have enough to eat, I'd wince and recede, when I desperately wanted to fall into her lap crying and expand.

When I feel like I truly have no one, I know on some level that's not as true as it once was. And the way I know that is often because of that stranger luck. Or when I'll get an email from someone who follows me on Twitter or Instagram, or someone who listens to It Was Romance, or someone who'll tell me I wrote something that really meant something to them. Or that Tinder Live made them laugh more than they've ever laughed in their life, or made them feel less alone in dating. Or when I go on tour and people tell me they'd always wanted to meet me which is just . . . as a lifetime loner this kills me in the best way. At any given moment, there could be someone out there reading my work or listening to It Was Romance records, and very often they'll want to message me so I know they felt seen, or that they see me and want me to feel as loved as I am. And I don't know what to do with it, other than beam and feel so held in that moment by someone I may never meet, but I'm working my way there.

Being alone is not a life sentence. I know it feels like it at the time, but I promise you, you will not be alone for the rest of your life. And if you are—which I am not going to say that'll never happen because I'm starting to see that maybe, in my own way, I will always be kind of alone—okay, let's see what happiness can be found there.

I've realized that sometimes being alone actually truly is better than being around people, especially if they're the wrong people. Sometimes you just need time to yourself and it doesn't make you weird or wrong. It's a sign you really like spending time with you, which is healthy as shit, so good job.

Giving yourself permission to hang out with yourself can absolutely be a gift if you can learn to see yourself as an ally, someone who got you through everything so far, whether it was totally alone or not. You know your whole story. You know everything. So believe yourself, validate yourself. Plus, even though movies and TV haven't accurately nailed the portrayal of this yet, you can have so much fun by yourself. List the things you'd want to do with other people. Go to the museum? Not a doubles activity. Go to a movie? Such a great thing to do alone. Tennis? Play against the wall. Especially if you don't have friends who make you feel safe and loved and heard and supported and special and great. It's absolutely better to be by yourself than with someone you don't even like, or whom you do like but they don't make you feel super great. Man, the number of times I went to parties I fucking hated with people who were jerks, even though I knew I'd have more fun by myself, even if that fun just meant sitting in a room alone silently is . . . too many times.

While most people hate sleeping alone, it's also important to note that sleeping in a queen- or king-size bed all by yourself is magnificent. Honestly, being able to sleep in any bed all by yourself is pretty fantastic, but in bigger beds you can really try some shit out. What if I slept diagonally so my whole body is across the bed? Ooooh. What if I slept so my head is where my feet should be? Ooooh. Man, I am good at having fun.

Bummed out about living alone? Here are some pros! When you are alone and living by yourself, no one cares if you do your dishes right away. Or put your shoes away immediately. Or really do anything involving cleaning if you don't want to. As someone who has had, like, thirty roommates in their life, I can tell you, this is really a thing to value. Along with solo dance parties, which truly are the best, most cathartic dance parties. Unless you are the person I aspire to be one day, you're never going to dance in public with the same reckless, carefree abandon that you have when it's midnight and you're in your room alone and your song comes on and you just go for it like you're in a movie montage.

Also, don't be too worried if you want to be alone a lot lately. Bamboo grows underground for three years before it sprouts up to thirty feet tall. Nothing blooms year-round, so if you need to be alone right now, that's what you need. And even if you fear that you're at the beginning of a depressive spiral that will ultimately lead to you failing at life because you can't be around people anymore, you're probably not. You probably just need a break and it's okay to take it. Plus, seeing all your friends regularly can be a fucking hassle. Everyone's busy, you're coordinating schedules, people are flaky. There's that one friend who always says, "We need to hang out!!!" and never tries or follows through and you're just, like, "Why do you even exist?" (in my life, not in the world, but still). It's so nice not having to worry about coordinating a bunch of other people. You want to go to an eleven a.m. movie? Just go. You don't have to check with anyone about shiiiiit.

One of my favorite alone things is to let myself be as weird as I want to be. Let's say I want to make the faces of all my friends using only potatoes and a series of Sharpies, while singing the entire *My Fair Lady* soundtrack in my underwear? I'm gonna go for it. Who's stopping me? No one.

I know sometimes being alone feels incredibly shitty and not empowering and is the worst. That's totally understandable! Being alone is sometimes incredibly painful. Feel how painful it is, know that feeling will pass, and you'll feel great again. It's hard to remind yourself of it in the moment, so just remind yourself of other times when life felt like way too much and like it would never feel great again, but it did, even for two seconds, even if it was just, like, "Oh, man, I love cookies." That counts. That's hope. Take it.

More than anything, know that you're never totally alone. We're all fed this idea that if we're not with our perfect person, or the perfect group of *Friends*-like friends (they weren't perfect, but you get what I mean) then we're totally alone. False: You have waiting room friends, or you have coworkers you make jokes with sometimes, or you have that cool old lady at the grocery who smiles at you every time she sees you. And all those people are glad you exist, even on the most basic level. Especially Grocery Store Gayle.

And listen, if you don't have IRL friends and all your friends exist on the internet? That's cool! Having online friends totally counts as having real friends, and for almost my entire life, online friends have been my lifeblood. But as I expand and allow myself to see I'm safer than I once was, this is a new world, it's okay, you can come out now, I see that all of the songs and jokes and shows and sketches and writing I've done has had a ripple effect. Because I wanted to help people feel less alone, they kindly mirrored that back to me by reaching out to tell me I wasn't alone either. I basically live on the internet (I'm trying to change this, but still, I love it), so if you're lonely, I'm probably posting jokes on Twitter or videos on Instagram because I love the internet and it is where my friends live, hooray the internet, etc.

That said, my internet friends often don't live here, and I'm not exactly going to reach out to someone who sent me one message about a *Cosmo* article to be like, "Hey, girl, what's up? Sooo I feel like dying. LOL for real, though!!!" In those moments, I cope in the ways I always have: putting on headphones and pretending I'm in a movie, or imagining I'm singing and dancing to the song onstage for fifty thousand people and we all feel connected for this one night. I go for "trash walks," in which I walk around an affluent neighborhood while keeping one eye peeled for the luxurious trash they leave on the street. (Laugh all you want, but I have a Cuisinart blender and a four-hundred-dollar iron and a million other things, the streets are littered with gold.) I go on Craigslist "free" and comb the treasures there. I go to restaurants and try new foods. I go on the playground swings at night by myself and sing as loud as I can while swinging. I take "night walks" where I go to parts of the city where no one is and I sing and dance in the streets so I'm not bothering anyone, but can also sing as loud as I want and dance as much as I want.

I found a gym I love that has a million classes per month and I go almost every day, because it's a quiet sense of community for sneaky weirdos. By that I mean, I go to all these classes, but I don't have to talk to anyone, no one knows who I am, but I get to see the teachers, and they tell me "Wow, you really understand this work!" when I do planks and I beam like the little kid who wasn't often told she was good at anything and laps up the encouragement like water on a 100-degree day. I love my gym classes because they focus on strength, not thinness, and most of all, I love that I can do things now in class that I couldn't do a year ago. It's a real-world confirmation that life can always get better, it can. Things that seem impossible for me to do or feel or have today could be totally different in six months. Knowing you truly can grow and change and be more than you think, in an easily measured way, just by showing up every day and trying, has been so healthy for me to see. I use the classes as an exercise in self-care more than anything, as a way to shift me from my pattern of "Do it, you piece of shit! Who cares if you're in pain? Just shut the fuck up and do it!" into something gentler.

So when I'm doing exercises, and everyone else is holding the plank for what seems like two hours, and after a minute, I don't want to anymore, I don't. It's the promise I made to myself when I signed up. That I would only do things that made me feel good and take breaks when I wanted to, no questions asked. And coming from a hard-core, lifelong, "bleed out on the street, or you're weak" person, that's huge. If I find myself getting in my head in yoga, I'll notice other people struggling in class and send them thoughts like "You got this! Just hang in there!" and hope it helps them through class. And when I'm holding a pose and I think, "I can't do this shit anymore. I'm gonna fuck it up!" I repeat, "I love you, I love you, I love you," in my head to replace that other voice that I DID NOT INVITE HERE!!!!

Sometimes I'll hold the door for people, or instead of grabbing one yoga block, I'll grab one for me and the person behind me, but I'm also very careful to not do too much of this because then I'm backsliding into I HAVE TO BE OF SERVICE TO EVERYONE OR ELSE I SHOULD DIE and that makes me feel way worse. On those days, my challenge is to receive, to let the door be held for me, to let someone give me their block, and not feel like I owe them $12,000 or I'm evil.

I was at my friend's house a few months ago and she offered me blankets on the couch because it was so cold outside. I said I was fine and didn't need one, nope. About an hour later, while she was bundled in layers and sweaters and multiple blankets, she said to me, "Dude, there's no way you're not cold. I'm wearing way more than you are and I'm covered in blankets and I'm still cold. Take a blanket." And I said, so terrified, "Okay." Once I took it, I began to cry. I told her my feet had been freezing and my hands were blue and I hadn't even noticed. That I wished I could be like her. She was cold, she got a blanket. She was thirsty, she got water. She had to pee, she didn't wait two hours until she was in physical pain and couldn't hold it anymore, which I've always done and only recently realized was weird when I told a friend, "Yeah, I've had to pee for, like, two hours," and they said simply, "Why???"

I told her I wished I could need something and my brain would register that and immediately fill that need. She looked at me and said, "Lane, I've always wanted to have an apartment where people could feel at home. It means the world to me that I have this couch and these blankets to give you so you can feel warm and comfortable. Because I'm so glad we're friends and I want you to feel at home here." Having never felt at home anywhere, I cried again. This time, at the idea that one day, maybe, I will.

Instead of trapping all these needs inside me, what if I expressed them, to the right people this time, and they were happy to meet them? I realized that recently when I was talking to a friend, Mary, whom, of course, I met through Instagram when she reached out to me to offer her home to me when I came to Tacoma with Tinder Live. She told me she knew it was probably weird because she was a stranger, but she'd love to have me stay with her while I was in town and also had a bunch of vintage clothes she was getting rid of that might fit me. I'm sure most people would see that and think it was nuts, but this is where my "Eh, fuck it, nothing's killed me yet!" comes in handy. This total stranger picked me up from the airport as promised, drove me to her beautiful house, and now we're friends. It's unconventional, but I think it's dreamy. I didn't get what most people got, sure, but man, what a cool, weird alternate life!

When we spoke recently, I was very depressed, and Mary asked what would help, and I said I didn't want to say, but then decided I did. "People always offer to buy you a beer or something and I don't want that. Can I be honest with you? Is that okay?" and she said it was. "I really just want someone to come over and brush my hair, or let me cry in their lap while they pet my head and tell me I'll be okay." And I cried harder because I felt so ashamed to want that from a friend, from someone who was not a romantic partner or a parent, because I didn't have either right now, but I still wanted it.

We section off physical comfort and intimacy so heavily. We reserve it for partners only, and platonic friends can only chitchat and that's it. How can you tell people to be okay with being single while also telling them they can only get the basic human needs of physical touch from not being single?

But then, TV characters cry in each other's laps, and race over with ice cream and hair braiding when someone so much as drops their car keys. And we're told this is normal and everyone but you has six loyal friends they see every single day. It's incredibly frustrating. So you take physical affection when you can get it, almost feeling guilty when you do. You might sleep with someone just to get to the cuddling part, knowing full well if the cuddling had been on the table, you might not have even slept with them to begin with. You might get super happy when your yoga teachers do adjustments because having someone touch you in a safe, gentle way, even for two seconds, feels like it changes your whole world. I know I do. Partly because human beings are designed to be physically comforted by one another, but also because it's soothing parental behavior I didn't often get as a kid. So when I get it now, it's the closest thing I can get to immediate happiness.

Mary didn't pause before saying, "Lane, I bet there are a ton of people near you who would love to do that for you. And next time you're in Tacoma, I would absolutely love to do that for you." And my tears went from light rain to waterfalls that kill people. I'd voiced a need and she didn't run away; she didn't think I was weird or too much. I still haven't asked anyone to do this, and my head remains unrubbed, but I'm a step closer than I was.

I watch people in groups a lot—at meditation centers, yoga classes, even my apartment building—and I know people want to work together. Our base nature is to be together, work together, help each other—and it's only removed once we have been hurt or denied that help from others, or had that desire ripped from us. But I know it's still there when people smile at you on the street, or hold the door for you when they didn't have to. It's still very much alive. So if you want to exercise that and feel close to people in a safe and slightly distant way, you can. Right now. Hold the door. Smile even though they might not smile back. Wish everyone on the train a good day in your head. Hug someone mentally. On the hardest, most brutal of days, even the smallest of kindnesses has gotten me through. So when you have the energy, do it. And in that, lonely as you may be in every other possible way, you are connected. Because I guarantee at least one person you affected will think of you all day, maybe even longer.

It may not be a Band-Aid, it may not be a salve, it may just be the equivalent of someone kissing your Band-Aid: an idea. A gesture. That, if you've ever put on Band-Aids yourself, with no kissing or well-wishing from anyone, can mean everything.

Be the person you've been waiting for. I know it sucks, but what's the alternative? Complaining about it? As much as I validate that life choice and find myself there often, it's exactly like falling down in the street and crying for someone to pick you up because you're in pain. It'd be great if they would. But they're your legs and you have to pick yourself up, or you'll just stay there forever.

Around Valentine's Day this year, I saw a posting online for an emergency foster needed for a rescue dog from Mexico and thought, "Hmm, maybe I could help this dog." But given that that same day, I felt more like giving up than I had in years, I laughed at the idea of that. "Okay, Lane, you can barely take care of yourself, but you can take care of a dog. Jeez, stop adding people/dogs in your life you have to take care of! Take care of yourself, please!" But I sent the email anyway, just to see. I'd wanted a dog since I was a teenager, thinking that adding a dog who could live in the car with me would be so fun and it'd be the two of us against the world, like *Oliver & Company*, but way sadder! But I never did anything about it, other than constantly google dog breeds who might do well in cars, because I figured it wasn't fair to the dog.

In the few months prior to seeing the post about the foster dog, I'd floated the idea in my own mind of allowing myself to have something I'd always wanted: a little sandy-colored Chihuahua in a denim vest with punk-rock patches who never barked and loved to cuddle but had super-mellow energy and was always super happy and never left my side. Everyone told me this dog didn't exist, that this was insane to want, and I figured maybe they were right, but I kept the dream alive, why not.

The rescue organization wrote back, I'd been approved. Whoa. Whoa. Whoa. I was not prepared for this. And with that, all of the reasons I hadn't gotten a dog prior surfaced: What if I wasn't rich enough to have a dog? What if I wasn't well enough? What if the dog is fucking evil? What if my apartment wasn't enough space for her and somehow she died because of that? What if I didn't know enough about dogs to be the perfect dog mom? What if I messed something up and hurt her by accident? I couldn't live with that! And what if, what if, what if. I called Mary, who has a dog, and she said, "Lane, if it's not a good fit, you give her back and she finds another foster." And I breathed deep and thought *okay*. I put a post online asking if anyone had any dog stuff because this dog was getting here tonight and I knew nothing, and people rallied. I went all over town to pick up bowls and toys and leashes and as much as I could before I went to pick her up at midnight from the woman who had flown her in from Los Angeles, after having been flown in from Mexico, where they'd found her at half of her weight, having been badly abused.

The girl got out of her car and handed me the dog carrier and I hopped in a cab with her on my lap. I wanted her to know she was okay, so I unzipped the top of her carrier and put my hand in so she could smell it, because then maybe she'd know I was safe. As soon as I put my hand in there, she laid her head in my hand like it was a pillow, like she was home. And I thought, "Oh, damn." And I just told myself it was nothing. All dogs do that to strangers probably. That night she slept curled up on my chest and never stopped smiling. She never barked, always looked happy, and was just as happy to sit on the couch with me while I worked as she was to go outside and play (well, eventually. She was terrified of the city for a while, which, same).

The next day I went to work and my roommate texted me, "I'm going to start calling this dog Little Lane. She's clearly damaged, but she's trying so hard to be a good dog." It was the truest thing said about me, and about her. Fostering doesn't allow for months of care, so I had to decide quickly if I wanted to keep her or if they should put her up for adoption. Having thought I'd get a dog when I got married or had a proper yard, years from now, I began to panic. I took her to get microchipped and the woman at the rescue organization said, "Are you thinking about keeping her?" and I said, "I think, maybe," and she said, "Well, dogs are a big commitment. How would you feel about having her for the next ten years?" and I said without thinking, "That's not enough time." I loved her already and it scared the shit out of me.

I came home that night and called everyone I knew, crying, panicked. Later, telling my roommate, "I hate the idea of anyone but me having this dog. She feels like my dog. But what if she's lying to me? What if she's secretly awful and cruel and she's just pretending she loves me so much because she wants something? Like, maybe she just wants food and one day she'll get comfortable with me and hate me and reject me and she'll leave or be mean to me and I'll be so sad. I know she's always smiling and so it *seems* like she really loves me, but what if she just does that to everyone?" My roommate laughed at how nuts I sounded, projecting all my lifelong fears about people, and surely about Max, onto this sweet little dog. He replied, simply, "Lane, the second you leave the house, she stops smiling. And all she does is sit on your couch, staring at the door, waiting for you to come back."

So I took a leap of faith that she was as great as she seemed. I took a leap of faith that maybe this unconditional love was as real as it seemed. And I adopted her. And I held her close and told her, "I am your family now and I will always be here, always, always. You have been through so much and you deserve the whole world. And I want to be the one to give it to you." Words I hope I one day hear from someone as well.

And I named her Lights. Partially, because I love the musician Lights so so much, but also because she was and is a beam of light that was brought into my life when I thought my life was over. In true romantic comedy fashion, she found me when I wasn't looking, and showed me true unconditional love I'd never known before.

Now she often sleeps curled up with her back on my chest, so I can put my arm around her little belly and spoon her while we sleep, smiling the whole time. Or with her back against my back, like she's a second spine. While I'm working, she'll just sit there and stare at me, smiling, while she watches me like she's letting me know I'm enough and she's so proud of me. When I work too much, she comes over and will push papers out of my hand, or press keyboard keys, like, "You've been working twelve hours, stoooop!!!"

I thought having a dog would be another example of my taking care of everyone but myself, but I quickly realized it was the opposite.

All the things I give to this dog—the twelve thousand times a day I tell her I love her and she's beautiful and special and perfect, all the belly rubs and dog massages I give her—are greatly appreciated, and that love is returned. And on the days when I can't do that as much, or I get wrapped up in work and forget, I always think she'll be mad at me, she'll hate me now, she'll leave. And she doesn't!!! That's a thing??? You can be not perfect and still be loved? THAT'S SO COOL!

Lights is everything I wanted in a dog, and people told me there's no way a dog like that existed, but she does. Which gives me faith the kind of partner I want can exist too. Looking at her burns and scars from everything she survived before I found her doesn't make her broken. I don't think of her as someone who "got what she deserved," I see her as someone who was around some very cruel people. She did nothing wrong, it was not her fault. And I am so honored that I get to make her feel loved and spoiled and adored every moment I possibly can for the rest of her life. And now I know it's possible that one day someone will look at me the exact same way, like they are so thrilled to be able to give me the life I should've always had.

And every time I have to feed her, it's a good reminder I have to feed myself too. Every time I have to take her outside, I probably needed to go outside too. A reminder to take care of her is a reminder to take care of myself. And to that end, I've started to, every time I tell her, "You are so beautiful, I love you so much, you are so special," I will add, "And I am so beautiful, I love myself so much, I am so special," because I need to hear it too. We all do.

At this point in time, I have no idea if I'll ever be someone who is super close to people and has a friend family and all of the things I thought I'd have by now, but I do know that every morning I wake up and I try to let people know how much I care for them, even if I don't feel like I belong to anything or anyone (except Lightsy, bless you, dog angel) in the way I want to yet, because I mean it. One of the perks of being alone this long, I guess, is I never want anyone to feel as awful as I have, even for a second. As long as I'm alive and breathing, I want to tell that girl in the park she looks beautiful today, I want to tell the girl who's crying on the subway I see her and it'll be okay, even if I can't guarantee that. I want to tell my friends they're special and deserve love and I will always be here for them, even if I'm not entirely sure they'll always, or even momentarily, be there for me. To me, the closest I've been able to get to not feeling alone is, at the very least, my hope that I can help people feel less alone too.

I still have fears that maybe I don't get a soul mate the way everyone else has them, maybe I don't get to belong the way I want to, I fucking hope not, but I'm still recovering right now and it can be hard to believe in. And if in the end I don't get that, then what? What is left?

And the only answer I have is that I am. Every now and then, when my anxiety takes me down the road of what would happen if I somehow lost everything, I remember that I am alive and I am free, even if my mind often makes me feel like I'm not. I get to eat really lovely food if I let myself. I can travel if I want to, even if it's two blocks away. I could go to the botanical gardens nearby and it's so peaceful and so pretty. I could dress up in some wigs and costumes if I wanted. I could sing at the top of my lungs or play one of my instruments. I'm alone, perhaps, sure, yes, but I'm here. I'm still fucking here.

And not in an "ugh, I'm still here" way, but in an "I am still around and there is still time for things to change" way. When I'm in a lot of pain, it's harder to believe things can change radically. But I know that I've gotten to a place where I'm texting with Janeane Garofalo, who meant more to me as a child than pretty much anyone, and doing Tinder Live with David Cross (whose stand-up albums and *Mr. Show* episodes were playing in my ears for most of my life, giving me hope that one day I'd be making comedy with other people who were like me, one day). Debbie Harry has heard me sing (!!?!!) and at one It Was Romance show, Parker fucking Posey told me my voice is incredible and that it "breaks the whole room wide open." PARKER POSEY QUEEN OF EVERYTHING SAID THIS TO ME IN REAL LIFE. Susie Lewis, co-creator of *Daria*, aka my child-hood lifeblood, told me she loved my web series. Rachel True from *The Craft* and I text about probiotics and tarot and swap dating advice and I more than happily tell her as often as possible that I think she's incredible, because one of the best things about getting to be friends with and meet my heroes is I get to tell them how much they meant to me before I even knew them. And it is so much. And if I'd have given up all the times I wanted to give up, look at what I would've missed.

I'm able to write things people want to read, and not only read like passive clickbait, but things that resonate with people and make a difference to them—the only kind of writing I ever gravitated toward, and the only kind of writing I ever wanted to do.

And career stuff aside, because maybe you're like, "Well, shit, I'm not remotely in that position," then throw that part out, who cares, it doesn't matter. My only point is that, in my wildest dreams, did I think a lot of the shit I have in my life now could happen to me? Totally, but only in my wildest dreams. So wild I knew they were very far away and had no idea how I would get there, or if I'd be alive long enough to see it happen.

But my point is, I think that's what you do. You book that trip for yourself, you take yourself to dinner and enjoy it the same as if someone else took you out. You take all that love you keep giving to selfish idiots and try to throw some of it in the general direction of your own heart and you pray even a little bit of it sticks there.

Maybe all that shit boomerangs around, maybe it doesn't. I can't know. But if everyone did it, we wouldn't feel alone ever. So be the idiot who cares too much, be the weirdo who makes a difference, be the person who, even if you never know it, kept someone from wanting to die because you smiled at them on the street. And in that way, in the smallest of ways, you're a little less alone. Because someone will remember you forever. In the way that I remember everyone who has ever been kind to me. I keep them all with me, so I know exactly where they are at all times.

But truly, as borderline depressing and kind of lame as it is, I'm a little less alone because you bought this book and you're right there, right now, being alone with me. And you should know I'd hug you if I could. So, so much. And I would tell you that you are loved and you matter and you are trying so hard. And that you deserve love and that any love you haven't received yet is waiting for you somewhere out there, and I know you're getting impatient and you're ready for it now, but it's coming, hold tight. And to not let the world and how it's been in the past make you cold and shut-down and scared, because it can just as easily be totally different tomorrow or the next day, it just could, just as I tell myself these things as often as possible.

There's so much I left out of this book because there was just too much to say and I didn't want to overwhelm you, or myself, in just one book. There are a comical number of personal traumas I couldn't lump into one book, so know the story of my past up until now is far from over, just like the story of my future hopefully is far from over.

But last time an elderly relative sent me a birthday card, she signed it the year I was born, then a dash, then 2018, like this is the year I die. So who fuckin' knows.

(Apparently she knows.)

ACKNOWLEDGMENTS

To Katy, without whom I don't know if I'd have been able to tell this part of my story or live to tell future ones. You will never know how much you have helped and how much less alone you made me feel. Thank you so much.

Thank you to my mom and my sister, for telling me this was my story to tell and fully supporting me in telling it. That means so much to me, as do you. I truly hope one day this pain and weight will be lifted from us all.

JL Stermer, thank you so much for believing I had books in me. Thank you for answering my exhausted and overwhelmed emails and replying with compassion and calming support. Thank you for not letting me give up on this book when I was in so much pain I didn't think I could write it. I cannot wait for the next fifty books you know I will probably start writing literally tomorrow.

To Laura Benanti, whom this book started with, when you introduced me to the wonderful Kat Brzozowski, who led me to JL Stermer, and now this book exists. I cannot tell you what you mean to me, Laura, on like eighty levels, but you mean so much.

To Jhanteigh Kupihea, for acquiring the book in the first place. And Rakesh Satyal, for getting me across the finish line.

To my New Leaf family, you are all so brilliant and magical, and I am so grateful to have you all in my corner.

To Josh Wynn and my Littlefield family, you have given me a sort of home and encouragement and support for Tinder Live that means so so so so much to me. I love you all so damn much it's crazy.

Cheryl Strayed, thank you so much for your words before I knew you and after. Your message to me in the last push of this book made me feel like I could survive it.

To Melissa, for always believing in me and for standing up for me in that shitty apartment. I'll never forget how great it felt to have someone have my back. And for sitting on the phone and editing this book with me in the last moments, in a way that was beyond helpful. I cannot wait for the world to read your words.

To Sean Lawton, for working so hard to bring Tinder Live around the world and for believing in me and my show just as much as I do, if not more. And to Darlene and Sophie and Braden and Mabel for being infinitely special people.

To Marcelle Karp and Trish Nelson, for being champions of women in comedy and two of the strongest, most incredible women I've ever known.

To Stacy London, for believing so devoutly in me and my potential, which has made it that much easier for me to believe in myself. You were one of my heroes as a kid and you are one of my heroes now.

To Angel, Ryan, and Lisa, thank you for believing in It Was Romance as much as I do and for being so stupidly talented, endlessly kind, and without any substance abuse problems. I feel all of that is pretty fucking special for a rock band.

To Sarah Thyre and Andy Richter, for being even funnier and kinder and more wonderful than I could've possibly imagined while watching you on TV as a kid. If possible, I admire you both even more now.

To Caissie St. Onge, for not only being a powerhouse but also for giving me a place to find myself again. You remain an idol in my eyes.

To Rachel True and Mara Wilson, for being childhood touchstones before I knew you, and adult touchstones now that I do.

To Nina Bargiel and Will Stegemann, for believing in me and being just incredible people.

To Jon Cryer, for being incredibly funny and kind and supportive, and perhaps most important, Duckie.

To Maris Kreizman, for being a very early reader of the book. I hope you like this version, which is radically different (cry laughing emoji) because I could not stop revising until I got it to where I knew it could go. You're wonderful.

To Phillia Kim Downs, for reviving my heart many times over with your magic.

To Dodai Stewart, for being a luminous boss who treats herself so well it inspires me to do the same.

To Toni and Beth and Jennifer, thank you for offering to be my family, and thank you for understanding why it is still so hard for me to let you.

To Alexandra Bolles, thank you so much for believing in me, even before we knew each other.

To Trish Bendix, Brittany Ashley, Laura Zak, Fawzia Mirza, and Lindsay Hicks, for seeing and believing in me and including me, and being my first LGBTQ family, all of which means the world. And to Lisa Donato, Christie Conochalla, and Lisa Tedesco, I cannot wait to make all of the movies with you.

To Akilah Hughes, for being my partner in crime. I cannot wait for everyone to see all the worlds we're building together.

To Sara Benincasa and Mandy Stadtmiller, for leading by example.

To Pia Glenn, Jennifer Pozner, Ellie Reed, Emmy Blotnick, Mike Drucker, Danny Gherman, Maressa Brown, and so many other friends, for sharing your own complicated family stories with me, so I could know how truly not alone I am and that this was a story worth telling.

To Nicole, Cristina, Sarah, and Annie, for giving me a respite and making me stronger.

To Nikitas Manikatos, Dustin David, and Ric Rosario, thank you for being my very first friend family, even though I see you guys once every like five years.

To Carol Heikkinen, for not only existing and creating one of my favorite films of all time but also for being kind and supportive and so damn funny.

And truly, to everyone who comes to every Tinder Live show, has been a guest on the panel, to everyone who buys my It Was Romance albums and comes to see us play music, and to everyone on Twitter and Patreon and Instagram and Facebook who wrote to me, supported me, and told me to keep going, and that this book would be great enough because it would be mine. You have no idea what you all mean to me.

ABOUT THE AUTHOR

Lane Moore is an award-winning comedian, writer, actor, and musician. The *New York Times* called her comedy show Tinder Live "ingenious." Her comedy and her band, It Was Romance, have been praised everywhere from *Pitchfork* to *Vogue*, and her writing has appeared everywhere from *The New Yorker* to *The Onion*. She is the former sex and relationships editor at *Cosmopolitan*, where she received a GLAAD Award for her groundbreaking work expanding the magazine's queer coverage. She lives in Brooklyn with her dog-child, Lights. Follow her @HelloLaneMoore on Instagram and Twitter or visit LaneMoore.org.